# GREAT BRITISH FOOD

10 9 8 7 6 5 4 3 2 1

Published in 2010 by Ebury Press,
an imprint of Ebury Publishing
Ebury Publishing is a division of the
Random House Group

The Random House Group Limited
Reg. No. 954009

Addresses for companies within the
Random House Group can be found at
www.randomhouse.co.uk

A CIP catalogue record for this book is
available from the British Library

Graphic design: Hudson-Powell
Copy editor: Norma Macmillan
Photography: Angela Moore
Styling: Sarah May

Photographs on p27 (bottom right)
and pp28–9 by Vanessa Lewis:
www.18thirty9.co.za

Photographs on p24 and p27 (top)
by Steve Theodorou:
theodorou@studio21photo.com

Photograph of the Too Many Cooks tea
towel (p30) reproduced by kind permission
of Robin and Lucienne Day.

The publishers would like to thank
Alexis at London Taxidermy, and Mark
at the Camping and Army Surplus Store
in Waterloo, who kindly donated the
gas stove.

The Random House Group makes every
effort to ensure that the papers used in
our books are made from trees that have
been legally sourced from well-managed
and credibly certified forests. Our paper
procurement policy can be found on
www.randomhouse.co.uk

Printed in China by C & C Offset
Printing Co., Ltd

ISBN: 9780091936327

To buy books by your favourite authors and
register for offers visit www.rbooks.co.uk

www.canteen.co.uk

CANTEEN

# GREAT BRITISH FOOD

EBURY
PRESS

## CHAPTER 1
## BREAKFAST AND ALL DAY

## CHAPTER 2
## STARTERS, SMALL DISHES
## AND SOUPS

## CHAPTER 4
## PUDDINGS AND DESSERTS

## CHAPTER 5
## CAKES AND BISCUITS

## CHAPTER 6
## BASICS AND MISC.

# SEASONAL BRITISH ALL-DAY DINING

## FOREWORD

The first time I reviewed Canteen, I went for breakfast and stayed for lunch. I was single on a Sunday morning, possibly the loneliest of all human conditions, and had nothing in the house to eat, let alone cuddle.

So I crawled into a pair of tracksuit bottoms and a holey jumper and slouched moodily off to Spitalfields for a fry-up at this new place I'd read about, which was taking the uber-trendy new British cooking and giving it to the people. They had got everything right in terms of provenance, principles and a party atmosphere, and it was said the plan was to gradually roll out a bit of a mini-chain.

In such a fashionable area, with such a modern food philosophy, I was half-fearing a restaurant high in concept but low in creature comforts: bony copywriters in fashion spectacles poking woodcock beaks and turnip tops around a square plate and listening to German techno on their iPods. But it was nothing of the sort, and I was blown away.

For here were toasted crumpets and butter, devilled kidneys, mushrooms on toast, potted duck with homemade piccalilli, welsh rarebit, hot buttered Arbroath smokies and macaroni cheese. And the place was warm and buzzy and full of families, contented solo eaters, and pretty girls. Everything you could ask for.

Within minutes, I had a great coffee in front of me – the sine qua non. And then I believe I had a single egg Benedict, with an egg Florentine on the side. And on the side of that, one of those crispy pucks of bubble and squeak they do, which I have now every time I go. And then, as noon came and the menu rolled over into lunch,

I had the roast rib of Charolais-Limousin from Sussex, sliced very thick and served pink and full of deep, beefy flavours, with exemplary Yorkshire pudding and potatoes roasted in duck fat.

And then, just when I thought it couldn't get any better, one of Canteen's founder heroes comes up to say hello, and it's Dominic Lake, my old pal from the Dome Café Bar in Hampstead, where we worked together as barmen in the early 1990s. I was already planning to be regular at Canteen, now it turned out I was family!

If Dom and I learned anything from our days at the Dome, it was just how a restaurant should not be run, and just what sort of food people should not be expected to eat. It is amazing to think how far London has come as an eating town since then, and the progress restaurants have made is nowhere exemplified better than at Canteen.

I've got the Baker Street branch now, which is much closer to home, so I'm a bit lazy about going into Spitalfields (or the Festival Hall). And now there is the recipe book, which you are holding in your hands. In theory, I can go through it page by page and make my own curried parsnip soup, steamed syrup pudding and spicy mutton pie. But that's not my style. I'm going to treat it as a menu. I'm going to drool over these stunning (and unusually funny and unpompous) pictures, thumb through the list of dishes until I find the one I fancy, and then get in the car and go down to Canteen and tell them to get on with it.

Giles Coren
London, 2010

## INTRODUCTION

Canteen is committed to providing honest food, nationally sourced, skilfully prepared and reasonably priced. We believe in good produce provenance. Our meat is additive-free, sourced directly from producers practising good animal husbandry and our fish delivered fresh from day boats on the South Coast. All dishes are cooked to order and the menu changes seasonally to accommodate the best and freshest national produce.

When we opened the first Canteen restaurant in 2005, in Spitalfields, London, we sought to offer reasonably priced, high-quality, modern British cooking in a welcoming environment that celebrated British craftsmanship and design. In all of this we think we have achieved our goal. There are now three more Canteens in London – in Baker Street, at the Royal Festival Hall on the South Bank and at Canary Wharf. All continue the Canteen philosophy of providing affordable honest food in well-designed, relaxing surroundings, throughout the day.

## COOKING

Canteen is often described as a stylish cross between a British transport caff and a diner, so it's not surprising to find sausages and mash with onion gravy, Scotch eggs, fish and chips, and fish cake with mushy peas on our menu. But ours are the best of the best and we hope you will try out our recipes.

Pies are our true signature dishes – we have made it our mission to resurrect our country's honourable tradition of savoury pastries. Inside their buttery pastry crust, our pies have savoury fillings made with the most appetising ingredients of the season. Steak and kidney, spicy mutton, and chicken and mushroom are perennial favourites. We always have a good selection of veggie pies too. In the restaurant our pies are served with mash, greens and proper gravy – this is our 'value meal' offered at a reasonable price.

There's always a daily roast on our menu – lamb, beef, pork or duck – as well as roast chicken, prepared and cooked at lunchtime and at dinnertime so they're fresh and succulent, never dried out. In the Roasts and Grills section you'll find recipes to show you how to cook these our way, as well as the essential sides and garnishes including proper gravy.

We're unapologetically nostalgic when it comes to our desserts and cakes. We truly believe that it's hard to beat treacle tart with clotted cream, crumble with custard, or home-made jelly and ice cream, especially with shortbread fingers. Our cakes and biscuits pay homage to all the prize-winners at village fêtes and WI fairs throughout the land.

## HISTORY

The three of us met at a time in our lives when we wanted to do something that was more rewarding. We were searching for a project that, of course, would be commercially successful, but at the same time one that we could feel passionate about. Pizza-pasta-noodle chains were ubiquitous in the UK, but it seemed to us that the food on offer was generally pretty poor. We thought we could take on the chains and offer an alternative of much higher quality.

In addition we felt that there was no good *British* food available on the high street. St John's (we are big fans of St John's) and Rules were just about the only traditional restaurants then – plus the odd gastropub – but they offer a particular kind of British food and can be quite exclusive. We decided that we wanted to offer something more egalitarian, more accessible (Canteen has been described as 'the Ivy cooking meets the Wagamama environment'). Part of our aim was to change the generally negative perception about everyday British food and traditional dishes.

In 2002/3, interest in food provenance was on the rise in Britain. It felt like just the right time to open a restaurant offering good, modern British cooking at reasonable prices, with well-produced food sourced from within these fair isles. The restaurant business should be an honest, workaday trade, rewarding, and simply about feeding people. It was a natural choice for us. This was the kind of business we wanted to start up.

We put together the initial concept and worked really hard on the business plan over two years, doing it just as the textbooks tell you, with lots of research into the market. Getting the finance for our first restaurant was the most stressful part of the process. We had to pitch to people with the power to make it happen – or not. It was a little like pitching to the investors on *Dragon's Den*, a nerve-wracking, tense time.

Running a restaurant is a complex business, and to be successful you need a good understanding of design, media and marketing, and complicated finance – not to mention food and cooking. We were restaurant outsiders, and as such we had to overcome resistance to our attempts to do things differently or try new technology and methods.

We hadn't envisaged our first restaurant being in a new building. But the site in the new development at Spitalfields Market turned out to be perfect – a bit of modernity in a historic London setting. It has worked well – we wanted a clean, clear environment that would be welcoming to everyone, of all generations – all-embracing. A modern version of the good old British works canteen, if you will, albeit a non-smoking one. We were very considered about the restaurant environment and design, aiming for longevity, not flash in the pan. We didn't want to embellish the menu too much either, and we put our mission statement at the top, so that our customers would know what we stand for.

We've been fortunate enough to have the support of many wonderful people who have helped spread the word from the beginning. We were busy from our opening day at Spitalfields, with queues snaking down the road, and within a few weeks we were serving up to one thousand customers a day.

## FOOD

The inspiration for our cooking is traditionally British – recipes from our country's culinary history, combined with comforting and familiar dishes from our own childhood. What are perceived to be 'classic' dishes are often hard to get right because it's tricky to please everyone – we all have our own idea of what a classic British dish should be. But at Canteen we've tried hard to provide the winning versions.

Canteen food is unpretentious but deeply flavoursome. We aim to let the freshness and quality of the ingredients be paramount. As you will see from the recipes in this book, we keep the preparation as simple and unfussy as we can.

Our menus change with the seasons, to offer British produce when it is at its best and freshest. Using fruits and vegetables when they are most delicious and abundant makes both the cooking and eating more enjoyably satisfying. We really don't long for asparagus during the winter, preferring to wait and anticipate those few weeks of an asparagus orgy in the spring.

All the dishes on our menu are cooked to order – everything is made from scratch in our kitchens, including our jams, piccalilli and cakes. It's really common-sense, economical cooking – true good housekeeping. Every dish tastes better when it's home-made. We think this is the way to cook, and the finest way to eat.

## GOOD PRODUCE PROVENANCE

Knowing the provenance of the food in our kitchen is important to us, and we source our food in the UK as much as possible, aiming to support British artisan producers. Every cook at home can follow the same ethic. But that doesn't mean you have to be sanctimonious – we know we couldn't do without ingredients like lemons and oranges, capers and olives.

At Canteen our meat and poultry comes from farmers who rear traditional breeds and practise good animal husbandry. It is free-range and additive-free, which we think is tastier and healthier to eat. We believe in using the whole animal, incorporating less familiar but very flavourful cuts in our dishes.

Safeguarding fish stocks is very much part of being environmentally responsible, so we use only what comes from sustainable sources. We buy our fish direct from small South Coast day-boats and what we put on the menu is dictated by that day's catch. It all depends on the vagaries of the British weather. Sometimes we find we have more unusual fish to cook, so we have learned to be flexible.

## WHO WE ARE

The founding partners of Canteen are Patrick Clayton-Malone, Dominic Lake and Cass Titcombe.

### PATRICK CLAYTON-MALONE

Patrick's interest in food stems from his upbringing in rural Dorset, and his mother's considerable influence at the kitchen table and in the back garden – where she grew fruit and vegetables, kept chickens, and made sauces, preserves and elderflower champagne. Visits to cattle markets and cake stalls at village fetes only enhanced his interest in the provenance and quality of what we eat.

Having left school at 16 after an illustrious academic career that majored on skateboards, music and girls, Patrick pursued a vocation in hospitality. Unfortunately he was fired from his first job as a kitchen porter in a Tex Mex restaurant. Falling back on those vital lessons learned while at school, Patrick began putting on parties in the Bath area. Organising an event for the Bath Fringe Festival led to a regular spot at the seminal club The Hub, where he booked internationally known artists such as Underworld, Roni Size and Propellerheads, and worked with cutting-edge record labels Wall of Sound and Skint.

Now earning the sort of money not often seen by Tex Mex kitchen porters, Patrick began to eat out regularly, and witnessed the discrepancy between the cheap but low-quality high-street brands and the fine-dining experience.

The continuing success of his music and event promotion led to the creation of a multimedia production company and ultimately to London. There, Patrick worked with Levi's, Orange, Gorillaz, Nokia, *i-D* magazine, Gap, *Dazed and Confused*, and MTV, and won a D&AD golden pencil for producing an innovative first online video ad campaign for Sony.

Meanwhile, the idea that had formed all those years ago back in Bath – that there could be a good-quality, British dining experience available for all – began to bear fruit. Patrick had met Cass years earlier, when the latter was a young chef in Bath. When the two of them met up again in London they began to plan a solution to the high-street malaise, and Canteen was born.

Patrick has taken a particular interest in developing the Canteen aesthetic. The Canteen Table design was instigated by him specifically for the restaurant, and its success prompted the realisation of another dream, his own design studio: Very Good & Proper (see p31).

### DOMINIC LAKE

One of four children, Dominic showed an entrepreneurial flare from a young age. While at secondary school he found an easy way to make money through re-selling cola cubes to his classmates, purchased in the morning then sold during the lunch break at a profit. A winning formula, thanks to children not being allowed to leave the school grounds at any time during the day.

Post-secondary school, Dominic tasted his first experience of catering when he took a job as a waiter at the infamous Dome in Hampstead, a part-time job he fulfilled whilst studying at Central St Martin's School of Art and Design (which he remembers as a time of brilliant fun).

Upon graduating, Dominic immediately put his creative skills to effective use when he designed and produced a 200-page mail order catalogue for a leading UK fashion packaging company. A similar challenge followed when he was asked to lead a retail turnaround project in central London, which he quickly brought back into profit. Having proven his obvious strengths in business, at the age of 30 Dominic was made investment executive at a boutique venture capital company. Throughout his burgeoning business career Dominic ensured he remained on top of his game through his MBA at the London Business School.

Having always held a flame for all things foodie, in 2001 Dominic architected the ultimate road trip for petrol-head and food lovers, and the European Motorcycle Extravaganza was created. Combining Europe's finest mountain roads with the best of Michelin-starred restaurants, including El Bulli, Les Prés d'Eugénie and Arzac, this taste-bud odyssey proved to be a huge success.

The desire to build on a passion for business and food, combined with a chance meeting with Patrick through one of his oldest friends, convinced Dominic that it was time for a change – Canteen was the end result.

### CASS TITCOMBE

Brought up around good food, Cass was reared on an entirely home-cooked diet in Wales. His parents fully embraced the self-sufficient lifestyle and one of his earliest memories is of sitting at the kitchen table, plucking the ends off blackcurrants for jam. The family grew and reared all their own ingredients, including chickens and ducks for eggs and goats for milk, aided by their own spring-fed well and a wind generator.

By the age of 10 Cass was plundering his mum's cookbook collection and taking it in turns with his siblings to cook the family meals. However, when the time came to start secondary school Cass was sent to a boys' comprehensive where, much to Cass's dismay, cooking was firmly off the curriculum.

Having left school at 16, Cass enrolled in a two-year catering course in Cheltenham. It was here that he landed his first job with a local catering firm. A move to Bath followed where he worked in a busy restaurant for two years, learning vital butchery skills with owner David Price, who bought all the meat on the carcass. It was while in Bath that Cass first met Patrick. In 1994 Cass moved to London to become chef de partie at Daphne's in South Kensington, where he was made sous chef within a year. Cass then went on to open the group's New York-style restaurant and bar, The Collection, then swiftly afterwards oversaw the opening of Pasha.

During his time at The Collection Cass realised that his passion lay with organic and seasonal food. In spring 2000 Cass moved to Italy with his partner and two children, Tabby and Oscar, and for four months travelled around the country developing a feel for simple, tasty cooking. On his return Cass settled in Brighton where he opened a small 30-cover restaurant. After 15 months there, he left to set up the Real Eating Company, where he ran the food operation for 18 months. It was at this time that Patrick introduced Cass to Dom and the Canteen plan was hatched.

## WHERE WE ARE

SPITALFIELDS

Spitalfields lies at the heart of the East End of London, an area of constant change and great diversity. Originally a Roman cemetery, Spitalfields is named after England's largest medieval hospital and priory, founded in 1197, which was known as St Mary's Spital. Most buildings in the area date from the mid-17th century, post-Great Fire of London. There are some great Georgian architectural gems here.

The original Spitalfields vegetable market was established in the 1680s, and has since moved further east. Today's stallholders in the market are a vibrant mix of food producers, antiques specialists and fashion designers. Canteen was one of the first eateries to move into Sir Norman Foster's new market building.

ROYAL FESTIVAL HALL

The Royal Festival Hall, built on the site of the Red Lion brewery on the south bank of the Thames, is the only permanent legacy of the 1951 Festival of Britain. Newly restored to its full Modernist glory, it is now looking better than ever and is the hub of cultural entertainment in the South Bank Centre, Europe's largest arts venue. You can enjoy music, art, film and theatre, including daily free promenade performances, as well as the London Eye, the world's highest observation wheel. Canteen is in a commanding position within the Royal Festival Hall itself.

BAKER STREET

London's Marylebone is a residential area of excellent Georgian housing with fantastic shopping, especially for food, fashion and design. Its name is derived from a medieval church called St Mary-by-the-Bourne, which was built on the banks of the Tyburn River. Within the Marylebone area is Baker Street, the setting for Sir Arthur Conan Doyle's Victorian detective stories. The study at 221b Baker Street (now a museum) is exactly as it was described in the Sherlock Holmes and Doctor Watson tales. Canteen is close by.

CANARY WHARF

In the late 1500s, the Port of London was alive with activity. Trade was expanding and Docklands became a point of departure for merchant ventures – in 1620 the *Mayflower* set sail from Rotherhithe to America. In 1802 the West India Docks opened and were considered to be the country's greatest civil engineering structure of its day. During the Second World War there were mass bombings of Docklands. But after the War, activity resumed and 1961 saw the peak year for the docks when over 60 million tons of cargo was handled. New technology and containerisation ended that success, and by the early 1970s most of the docks had closed.

In 1980 planning for the regeneration began, aimed at encouraging people to return to live and work in the area. Today, London Docklands stretches eight miles eastwards from Tower Bridge. It has its own transport system with the Docklands Light Railway, Britain's first-ever automated light-rail transit system, and London City Airport, as well as magnificent office and residential buildings, restaurants and hotels, and it has become a major shopping destination for Londoners. Canteen is in the exciting new glass Park Pavilion next to One Canada Square, the tallest building in Britain.

## DESIGN

In the months prior to the opening of the first Canteen in Spitalfields Market, I was picking up little snippets of information regarding the imminent launch of a no-nonsense British restaurant concept with an exacting design brief. Working on the project was a pedigree list of designers and suppliers, including quality furniture makers Windmill Furniture, architectural practice Universal Design Studio, graphic designers Hudson-Powell and leading design retailer Twentytwentyone. My eyes and ears pricked up.

All too often in my experience, dining establishments promise too much with their interiors, the grandeur of which doesn't deliver in the food and service departments. Fortunately, a lunch invitation would provide me with first-hand experience of how well the design has been integrated into the overall restaurant experience. Every opportunity was there for me to pick apart particular design details and hear them instantaneously rationalised by the creators. I was in for a potentially exhausting lunch of pure design geekery.

As it transpired, after a customary lap around the restaurant, we only talked about the design for about ten minutes before placing our orders and tucking into a jovial mid-week feed with plenty of banter.

The reason for this is simple. In the best way possible, the design needed no explanation or justification. It is devoid of any poetic fanfare or puzzling decorative features. It is entirely new and bespoke but feels comfortable and familiar. The space is functional, even utilitarian, but most certainly not stark or austere. By contrast, it feels positively cosy and intimate which is brought about through the use of warm, tactile, high-quality materials such as oak, cork, Portoro marble and Corian coupled with low-level lighting. Low-slung booth seating creates focused table settings suitable for either a business meeting, lunch with gran, or a romantic sojourn alike.

Dining here feels informal yet still possesses a sense of occasion. The honest material palette gives it a timeless appeal that succeeds at attracting customers of all ages. The layout feels democratic. Large communal 'Home' tables (existing classics by Barber Osgerby) occupy the central core where group gatherings enjoy massive feasts. The references are clear – from eating houses and libraries to schools and working mens' caffs – this restaurant subtly amplifies the best qualities of them all.

The owners cite their motivations for the restaurant including some examples of mid-century modernist interiors. Indeed, there are some hints of nostalgia that no doubt add to the charm, appeal and intimacy of this restaurant, perhaps accented in the identity and use of fonts that feel modern yet reminiscent of post-war, ration book utility. Retro, however, is a word to avoid here.

Importantly, the interior is harmonious with the sort of food that is served here – honest, straight up, comforting and considered. The balance between food and design is perfectly level and most importantly for me, the design attracts but it does not distract. With four restaurants now in the mix, each with their own characteristics, consistency has nonetheless been perfectly upheld.

Max Fraser

Canteen invites you to celebrate our opening
November 29th 2005 *7pm–10pm* P
RSVP Lisa Ispani *lisa@canteen.sera.com*
020 7034 0200 A feasting buffet will be served
throughout the evening

## VERY GOOD & PROPER

In 2008, in conjunction with the launch of Canteen's Baker Street restaurant, a new product design and production company was unveiled by Canteen co-founder Patrick Clayton-Malone. Named Very Good & Proper, the business debuted off the back of the Canteen Table, which was designed specifically in response to a need for the new restaurant.

The commissioning of bespoke furniture in the fit-out of restaurants is not a new concept, particularly at the high-end of the market where such establishments call for a tailored interior to mirror the craftsmanship of their kitchen and the quality of their service. However, the connotation of a canteen is one of democracy and mass-manufactured utilitarianism. With that in mind, the creation of a new table for this restaurant would need to align more closely with the egalitarianism of proper industrial production, both aesthetically and conceptually.

The initial design brief was to develop a cost-efficient table solution with café, bistro, and formal dining applications. To achieve this, the talents of design duo André Klauser and Ed Carpenter were called upon. The key design feature that they integrated is the elegant cast aluminium leg which fixes directly to the birch ply tabletop without the need for a bracing system. The table is quick and simple to put together and easy to dismantle and store. The leg, which can in fact be attached to any tabletop, is slender yet sturdy in its construction – its profile inspired by the cast iron brackets that held up Victorian cisterns, as well as the leg profile of Ernest Race's 'BA' chair from the 1950s.

At the Canary Wharf restaurant, the Canteen Utility Chair, a new addition to VG&P in 2009, joins the table. This design is a contemporary interpretation of the ubiquitous post-war school chair, made from a powder-coated steel frame and a pressed beech plywood seat and back.

Furthermore, a smaller item in the form of the Canteen Hook & Knob, also joins the collection – made simply from a powder coated steel backplate and hook with a large round aluminium knob holding it to the wall.

The idea that a restauranteur would take commissioned designs beyond the confines of the restaurant and launch it as a commercially available product is certainly unusual, but in this case entirely appropriate. For Clayton-Malone, good design in his restaurants isn't simply a means to an end but absolutely integral to the overall food experience. In truly democratic Canteen style, it is no wonder he also wants to make the VG&P collection more accessible to all.

Max Fraser

Max Fraser is the author of *London Design Guide* (opposite right), Max's first solo venture into print publishing, produced under his imprint Spotlight Press. www.londondesignguide.com

The VG&P collection is available through design retailer Twentytwentyone, a specialist design retailer known for the quality of their product selection and for working with renowned designers including Lucienne Day (Too Many Cooks tea towel, opposite left). www.twentytwentyone.com, www.verygoodandproper.co.uk

CHAPTER 1

# BREAKFAST AND ALL DAY

## PORRIDGE

*Serves 1*

We have porridge on the menu during the winter, but it seems many people like it year round – when we take it off in May we get a lot of complaints. Maybe that's because in a typical British summer a sustaining bowl of creamy oats is a comfort.

**50G ROLLED OATS**
**225ML FULL-FAT MILK**
**PINCH OF SALT**

TO SERVE
**COLD MILK AND BROWN SUGAR**

1. Put the oats and milk with a pinch of salt into a saucepan on a medium heat. Bring to the boil, stirring frequently. 2. Cook for a few minutes, stirring occasionally, until the porridge thickens and is glossy. 3. Pour into a bowl and serve with cold milk and brown sugar.

NOTES: For best results use one measure oats to two measures liquid. If you have American cup measures, ½ cup oats to 1 cup liquid is perfect for one portion • We prefer milk but you can use water or any other dairy-free alternatives to make porridge – even single cream if you want it really decadent • Try adding some chopped banana at the end and serving with honey.

## ROAST TOMATOES ON TOAST

*Serves 4*

In the summer months, when tomatoes are sweet and flavoursome, this makes a great snack any time. Plum tomatoes are the best ones to use – preferably those that are vine-ripened in the sun – because they keep their shape when roasted.

**12 PLUM TOMATOES**
**4 GARLIC CLOVES**
**75ML OLIVE OIL**
**A FEW SPRIGS OF FRESH THYME**
**SALT AND BLACK PEPPER**

TO SERVE
**4 THICK SLICES WHITE**
**SOURDOUGH BREAD**
**OLIVE OIL TO DRIZZLE**

1. Preheat the oven to 140°C. Halve the tomatoes lengthways. 2. Finely chop the garlic and mix with the olive oil in a large bowl. 3. Add the tomatoes and thyme. Season with black pepper and mix gently together to coat all of the tomato halves with oil. 4. Lay them out cut-side up on a baking sheet. Roast for 1 hour. 5. Remove from the oven and sprinkle with salt. 6. Toast the bread. 7. Place 6 tomato halves on each piece of toast and drizzle a little more olive oil over the top.

NOTES: You can use slices of multigrain bloomer instead of sourdough • If roasting the tomatoes ahead of time, warm them gently under the grill before serving • Fresh marjoram can replace the thyme, or freshly chopped basil sprinkled on the tomatoes just before serving.

## RHUBARB COMPOTE WITH YOGHURT AND GRANOLA
*Serves 4*

Forced or champagne rhubarb from Yorkshire's 'rhubarb triangle' (where it grows in the dark and is harvested by candlelight) has slim, tender stems with a sweeter flavour than rhubarb grown outdoors. If you are using outdoor rhubarb for this compote and the stems are large and fat, it's best to peel them.

**400G FORCED HOTHOUSE RHUBARB**
**75G CASTER SUGAR**
**A FEW THIN SLICES OF FRESH GINGER**
**PARED ZEST AND JUICE OF 1 ORANGE**

TO SERVE
**THICK GREEK YOGHURT**
**GRANOLA OR MUESLI**

**1.** Preheat the oven to 150°C. Wash the rhubarb and cut into 2cm chunks. Put into a stainless steel ovenproof pan with a lid. **2.** Add the sugar, sliced ginger, and orange zest and juice. Toss together and cover the pan. **3.** Place in the oven and cook for 30–40 minutes until the rhubarb is just tender when tested with the tip of a knife. Allow to cool. **4.** Serve with yoghurt and granola or muesli.

NOTES: You can store the rhubarb compote in the fridge until needed • If you make more, you will have some for a trifle (p177).

## WELSH RAREBIT
*Serves 4*

The Welsh version of cheese on toast is a favourite snack. But is it correctly called rarebit or rabbit? Apparently rabbit was used first. Perhaps that was thought to be too downmarket for such a fine dish?

**100ML MILK**
**50ML PALE ALE**
**25G BUTTER**
**25G PLAIN WHITE FLOUR**
**150G MONTGOMERY'S CHEDDAR, OR OTHER MATURE CHEDDAR OF YOUR CHOICE, GRATED**
**2 TSP WORCESTERSHIRE SAUCE**
**1 EGG YOLK**
**2 TBSP GRAIN MUSTARD**
**4 THICK SLICES BROWN BREAD**

**1.** Preheat the grill. Warm the milk and ale together in a saucepan. **2.** Melt the butter in another saucepan, then add the flour and cook for 2 minutes, stirring. Whisk in the hot milk mixture and cook until bubbling, whisking constantly until smooth and glossy. **3.** Remove from the heat. Beat in the cheese, followed by the Worcestershire sauce, egg yolk and grain mustard. **4.** Toast the bread on both sides under the grill. **5.** Spread over the cheese mixture, right to the edges. Grill until golden brown and bubbling.

NOTES: This is best on slices from a nutty brown loaf • Try using different cheeses, such as Lancashire or Caerphilly • Guinness is a good alternative to pale ale, for a richer mixture • Great with a poached egg on top to make a Buck Rarebit • The cheese mixture can be made in advance and kept in the fridge.

## HOT BUTTERED ARBROATH SMOKIE
*Serves 1*

We get our smokies from Alex Spinks in Arbroath, where they prepare them in the traditional way. These small hot-smoked haddock are so succulent, with a wonderful mellow flavour, that they need little embellishment. Butter and lemon are just fine.

**1 ARBROATH SMOKIE**
**25G SOFT BUTTER**
**1/2 LEMON**

TO SERVE
**A HANDFUL OF WATERCRESS SPRIGS TOSSED WITH SHERRY VINEGAR DRESSING (P207)**
**BREAD AND BUTTER**

1. Preheat the oven to 200°C. Cover the smokie with soft butter and place in a small tin. 2. Bake for 7–8 minutes until it is piping hot. 3. Transfer the smokie to a warm plate. Pour over any butter left in the tin. 4. Garnish with the lemon and serve with a watercress salad and bread and butter.

## CANTEEN PLOUGHMAN'S
*Serves 1*

The traditional basic ploughman's – bread, cheese and pickle – makes a sturdy, simple lunch, but as with all simple things the quality of the component parts is important. For their exceptional quality, we use British artisan cheeses from Neal's Yard, and add some apple and celery for crunch.

**CHEESE OF YOUR CHOICE – AS MUCH AND AS MANY DIFFERENT KINDS AS YOU LIKE**
**1 EATING APPLE, HALVED AND CORED**
**SLICES OF GRANARY BREAD**
**CELERY CUT INTO SHORT STICKS**
**CHUTNEY OR PICKLE (SEE BELOW)**

Arrange all the elements of the ploughman's on a large plate and enjoy.

NOTES: Try Apple or Pear chutney (p209), Piccalilli (p210), Beetroot relish (p209) or Pickled shallots (p208) in the Ploughman's • Cheese should always be served at room temperature for best flavour. Take it out of the fridge at least half an hour before serving.

## EGGS FLORENTINE
*Serves 4*

Both this and eggs Benedict are popular throughout the day, not just for breakfast or brunch, no doubt because of the perfect combination of ingredients – poached egg and spinach or ham on an English muffin, topped with buttery hollandaise. Our muffins are handmade by Flour Station, which you will find at a lot of farmers' markets.

**50ML WHITE WINE VINEGAR**
**8 EGGS**
**4 ENGLISH MUFFINS**
**1 QUANTITY HOLLANDAISE SAUCE (P203)**

SPINACH

**OLIVE OIL**
**500G SPINACH**
**FRESHLY GRATED NUTMEG**
**FRESHLY GROUND BLACK PEPPER**
**20G BUTTER**

1. First prepare the spinach. Heat up a pan large enough to hold all the spinach. When it is very hot, add a splash of olive oil and throw in the spinach. Turn it over with tongs for 1–2 minutes until wilted.
2. Tip into a colander and press out any excess liquid. Return to the pan and season with a few gratings of nutmeg, pepper to taste and the butter. Divide into four portions. Keep warm. 3. Preheat the grill. To poach the eggs, bring a pan of water to the boil and add the vinegar. When simmering, gently crack the eggs and slip them into the water, without breaking the yolks. Poach the eggs for about 3 minutes or until the whites are set but the yolks are still soft. 4. Meanwhile, split the muffins and toast them on both sides under the grill. 5. Put a portion of spinach on each muffin half and warm under the grill.
6. When the eggs are done, lift them out on a slotted spoon and pat dry with kitchen paper. Place one on each muffin half and spoon over the hollandaise.

NOTE: For Eggs Benedict, instead of spinach, top each toasted muffin half with a slice of high-quality smoked ham.

## SCOTCH EGGS
*Makes 6*

The Scotch egg in most pubs and supermarkets is a sad affair. Ours, though, is a proper Scotch egg, made with a free-range organic egg, the yolk just set, wrapped in a generous sausage meat coat. It makes a great snack or starter to share. Delicious with piccalilli as well as salad cream (see p206 for a recipe).

**7 MEDIUM EGGS**
**500G PORK SAUSAGE MEAT**
**BIG PINCH EACH OF GROUND**
   **ALLSPICE, MACE AND WHITE**
   **PEPPER**
**10 FRESH SAGE LEAVES, FINELY**
   **CHOPPED**
**WORCESTERSHIRE SAUCE**
**PICCALILLI (P210) TO SERVE**

COATING AND FRYING
**PLAIN WHITE FLOUR**
**1 EGG, BEATEN WITH THE SAME**
   **QUANTITY OF MILK**
**ABOUT 200G DRIED WHITE**
   **BREADCRUMBS**
**SUNFLOWER OIL**

**1.** Bring a pan of water to the boil. Place six of the eggs in the water and cook for 7 minutes. Drain and immerse in cold water. When the eggs are cool, peel them. **2.** Combine the sausage meat, spices, sage, a few splashes of Worcestershire sauce and the remaining egg. Mix well. Divide into six portions. **3.** Take one portion of the sausage meat and flatten on your hand. Coat one cooked egg in flour, then wrap the meat around it, moulding it into a nice egg shape. Make sure there are no holes in the sausage wrapping. Repeat with the rest of the eggs and sausage-meat portions. **4.** Coat first in flour, then dip into the beaten egg and, finally, roll in breadcrumbs to coat evenly all over. **5.** Heat a deep pan one-third full of sunflower oil to 160°C. Deep-fry the Scotch eggs for about 6 minutes or until the coating is golden brown and crisp. **6.** Drain on kitchen paper and allow to cool slightly for 5–10 minutes before cutting into wedges. Serve with piccalilli.

NOTE: If you wet your hands slightly first, it will be easier to shape the sausage-meat mix around the egg.

## SAUSAGE ROLLS
*Makes about 30*

Our sausage rolls are small – one- or two-bite size – and we think they work well as a little sharing snack before dinner. The sage, apple and onion give a nice, slightly sweet edge to the traditional sausage filling. A good dip to go with these is a mix of tomato ketchup and English mustard.

**I MEDIUM ONION, FINELY DICED**
**2 TSP SUNFLOWER OIL**
**200G PORK SAUSAGE MEAT**
**100G GRATED EATING APPLE**
**8 FRESH SAGE LEAVES**
**BIG PINCH OF GROUND MACE**
**BIG PINCH OF GROUND ALLSPICE**
**BLACK PEPPER**
**500G PUFF PASTRY SHEETS,**
 **IDEALLY MADE WITH BUTTER**
**2 EGG YOLKS, BEATEN**

**1.** Sweat the onion in the oil until soft, then allow to cool. Combine with the sausage meat, apple, sage, spices and some black pepper and mix together well with your hands. **2.** Preheat the oven to 170°C. Lay the puff pastry out on a worktop. Cut the pastry across its width into three strips about 8cm wide. **3.** Divide the sausage meat mixture into three portions and squeeze each one into a tube shape the same length as the pastry strips. **4.** Lay a tube of sausage meat on each pastry strip. Very lightly brush the long pastry edges with beaten egg yolk, then wrap them over the sausage, overlapping the pastry edges. Dip a fork in flour and press on to the join to seal. **5.** Cut each long sausage roll across into 3cm lengths. Place on a baking sheet, ensuring they are not touching each other. Brush them with beaten egg yolk to glaze. **6.** Bake for about 20 minutes or until the pastry is puffed and golden brown. Allow to cool. If not serving straight away, keep in the fridge until needed.

NOTE: Puff pastry is usually best when hot. So if you want to make the sausage rolls ahead of time, reheat them in a 175°C oven for 5 minutes before serving.

## BUBBLE AND SQUEAK
*Serves 4*

We think of bubble and squeak as being a way to use up leftovers, but originally it was quite a posh dish made with beef and cabbage. For our version we fry the bubble in meat drippings, and use potatoes that have been roasted in duck fat, to give a delicious savoury meatiness.

**500G LEFTOVER DUCK-FAT ROAST POTATOES (P130)**
**ABOUT 150G LEFTOVER COOKED CABBAGE OR OTHER GREENS**
**LEFTOVER FAT FROM ROAST BEEF, PORK OR DUCK**
**SALT AND BLACK PEPPER**

TO SERVE
**12 RASHERS DRY-CURE STREAKY BACON**
**VEGETABLE OIL**
**8 EGGS**

1. Preheat the grill. Coarsely crush the potatoes with your hands. Chop the cooked cabbage. 2. Heat up 2–3 tablespoons fat in a large frying pan. Add the potatoes and cabbage and cook for 3–4 minutes, mixing well with a wooden spoon. Season with black pepper and salt, if needed. Remove from the pan to a bowl. 3. Cool the vegetable mix until you can handle it, then divide into four and shape into rounds that are about 8cm diameter and 3cm thick. A good way to get neat shapes is to use a large pastry cutter or metal ring. 4. Heat up the frying pan and add a little more fat. Put in the bubble rounds and fry over a medium heat for 3–4 minutes on each side until golden and crisp. 5. While the bubble rounds are frying, grill the bacon until crisp. 6. When the bubble is ready, keep warm in a low oven. Heat up some vegetable oil in the frying pan on a low heat and fry the eggs until just set (about 2–3 minutes). 7. Place the bubble on plates and top each with three bacon rashers and two fried eggs.

NOTES: You can also make this with half roast potatoes and half mash · If you don't have any leftover fat from a roast, use duck or goose fat.

## BABY SPINACH, BACON AND POACHED EGG SALAD
### *Serves 4*

This is our healthy version of a fried breakfast. Rather than frying, the bacon is grilled, the bread is baked and the egg is poached, then all are combined in a salad. A delicious way to start the day that doesn't leave you feeling too full – or guilty.

**8 RASHERS DRY-CURE STREAKY
  BACON
3 TBSP WHITE WINE VINEGAR
4 EGGS
250G BABY SPINACH**

MUSTARD DRESSING
**1 1/2 TSP DIJON MUSTARD
1 1/2 TSP WHITE WINE VINEGAR
1 SMALL GARLIC CLOVE, FINELY
  CHOPPED
50ML RAPESEED OIL**

CROUTONS
**3 SLICES WHITE SOURDOUGH
  BREAD, CRUSTS REMOVED, CUT
  INTO 1.5CM CUBES
4 TSP OLIVE OIL
20G BUTTER, MELTED
SALT AND BLACK PEPPER**

**1.** First make the dressing. Whisk the mustard with the vinegar, 1½ teaspoons water and the garlic. Slowly add the oil, whisking to make a thick emulsion.
**2.** Preheat the oven to 170°C. Toss the cubed bread with the olive oil and butter. Spread out on a baking sheet. Bake for about 10 minutes or until golden brown. Season the croutons with salt and pepper.
**3.** Preheat the grill and grill the bacon until crisp, then crumble it. **4.** Heat up a large, wide pan of water and add the vinegar. When simmering, gently crack the eggs and slip them into the water, without breaking the yolks. Poach the eggs for about 3 minutes or until the whites are set but the yolks are still soft. **5.** Meanwhile, toss the spinach with the dressing and croutons. Divide among four plates and scatter the bacon over the top. **6.** Lift out the eggs on a slotted spoon and pat dry with kitchen paper. Place one egg on each salad and serve.

NOTE: You can make this with watercress sprigs instead of spinach.

## DEVILS ON HORSEBACK
*Makes 16*

At one time a highly flavoured mouthful like this – a sweet prune wrapped in salty bacon – would have been served as the savoury course after the sweet at grand dinners in country houses. We offer these 'savouries' as a snack to be enjoyed at any time.

**8 RASHERS DRY-CURE STREAKY BACON**
**16 STONED PRUNES**

1. Preheat the oven to 175°C. Cut the rashers of bacon across in half. 2. Wrap each prune in bacon and skewer with a wooden cocktail stick. 3. Place on a baking sheet and cook in the oven for 15–20 minutes until the bacon is golden and crisp. Serve hot.

NOTE: You can wrap other small bites in bacon and cook in the same way. Try bite-size pieces of kidney – Devilled kidneys (p65), cut in quarters – or freshly shucked oysters. Oysters in bacon are known as Angels on horseback.

## CHAPTER 2

# STARTERS, SMALL DISHES AND SOUPS

## ROAST SQUASH AND FENNEL WITH SPELT
*Serves 4*

Our friend and colleague Timothy Mawn, who was head chef at the Spitalfields Canteen, came up with this recipe when devising a new non-dairy vegetarian dish for the menu. Spelt grain has a nutty flavour that works really well with sweet butternut squash and aromatic fennel.

I LARGE FENNEL BULB
   (ABOUT 300G)
500G BUTTERNUT SQUASH
4 BAY LEAVES
4 GARLIC CLOVES, LEFT WHOLE
   AND BASHED
JUICE OF 1/2 LEMON
50ML OLIVE OIL
SALT AND BLACK PEPPER

SPELT

2 TBSP OLIVE OIL
50G CELERY (ABOUT I LARGE
   STICK), FINELY DICED
40G FENNEL, FINELY DICED
40G LEEKS, FINELY DICED
2 GARLIC CLOVES, FINELY
   CHOPPED
100G PEARLED SPELT
300ML VEGETABLE STOCK
   (SEE P202, NOTE)

DRESSING

20G FRESH MARJORAM LEAVES
JUICE OF 1/2 LEMON
4 TBSP OLIVE OIL

1. Preheat the oven to 180°C. Cut the fennel into wedges. Peel the butternut squash and remove the seeds, then cut into similar-size wedges. Place the vegetables in a roasting tray. Tuck in the bay leaves and garlic. 2. Squeeze the lemon juice over the vegetables and drizzle with the olive oil. Toss the vegetables so they are all are covered with oil. Season with salt. 3. Roast for 20–25 minutes until the vegetables are lightly browned and just tender but not mushy. 4. Meanwhile, prepare the spelt. Heat the oil in a medium saucepan and sweat the celery, fennel, leeks and garlic for about 5 minutes or until soft and translucent. Add the spelt and cook for a further 2 minutes, stirring. 5. Pour in the vegetable stock and add a pinch of salt. Bring to the boil and simmer for 6 minutes. Remove from the heat, cover with a lid and leave for at least an hour, to allow the spelt to absorb the liquid and become tender but still firm. 6. To make the dressing, chop the marjoram. Whisk together the marjoram, lemon juice and olive oil in a large bowl. Add seasoning to taste. 7. Add the roasted vegetables and spelt to the dressing and toss together. Check the seasoning. Allow to cool slightly before serving warm or at room temperature.

NOTE: You can use pearl barley instead of spelt.

## CHICORY, PEAR AND CASHEL BLUE SALAD
*Serves 2*

This quickly made dish has been on our menu since the beginning. We like to use Cashel Blue cheese because it is creamy and not too blue, but you could substitute any blue cheese you fancy. Serve this with some good bread.

**300G CHICORY**
**100G CASHEL BLUE CHEESE**
**2 TSP SHERRY VINEGAR DRESSING (P207)**
**10G FRESH CHIVES, CUT INTO 1CM PIECES**
**1 RIPE BUT FIRM PEAR**
**40G SKINNED ROASTED HAZELNUTS**
**BLACK PEPPER**

1. Cut off the root end of the chicory and separate the leaves, keeping them whole. 2. Remove any skin from the cheese, then cut into small cubes. 3. Place the chicory leaves in a mixing bowl and toss with the dressing, chives and cheese. Season with black pepper. Transfer to a shallow serving bowl. 4. Cut the pear into quarters and remove the core. Cut into thin slices and scatter over the salad. 5. Crush the nuts in a clean tea towel using a rolling pin. Sprinkle over the salad and serve.

NOTE: For a different twist, replace the Cashel Blue and hazelnuts with Stilton and walnuts.

## BEETROOT WITH HORSERADISH
*Serves 2*

Most people throw away beetroot leaves, which is a shame as they really are delicious, with a pleasant, slightly curry-leaf flavour. This is great as a light dish with some good bread and butter, or as an accompaniment to beef.

**1 BUNCH SMALL BEETROOT WITH LEAVES**
**1 TBSP OLIVE OIL**
**1 GARLIC CLOVE, FINELY CHOPPED**
**SALT**
**40G HORSERADISH SAUCE (P137)**

1. Remove the beetroot leaves and reserve. Wash the beetroot, then put them into a pan, cover with cold water and bring to the boil. Cook until just tender (about 30 minutes) – stick a knife into the beetroot and lift it out of the water; if it falls off the knife it is ready. 2. Drain and run under cold water. Rub off the skins. Trim off the ends, then cut the beetroot into wedges. 3. Wash the leaves. Discard the stalks and shred the leaves. 4. Heat up a frying pan with the olive oil and fry the garlic for 1–2 minutes until golden. Throw in the beetroot wedges followed by the leaves. Toss the vegetables over a medium heat for another 1–2 minutes until the leaves are just wilted. Taste and add salt if necessary. 5. Serve each portion with a dollop of horseradish sauce on top.

NOTE: Make sure the beetroot leaves are fresh and bright without any discoloration.

## ROAST TOMATO AND GOAT'S CHEESE TART

*Serves 6*

This is a nice summer dish. The contrast of crunchy pastry case and creamy filling is a good mouthful, and the tomatoes cut through the richness of the cheese and cream perfectly.

- **100G SOFT, CREAMY GOAT'S CHEESE**
- **25CM SHORT PASTRY CASE, BAKED BLIND (P207)**
- **15G FRESH BASIL LEAVES**
- **12 ROAST TOMATO HALVES (P36)**
- **250ML DOUBLE CREAM**
- **5 EGG YOLKS**
- **SALT AND BLACK PEPPER**

**1.** Preheat the oven to 135°C. **2.** Remove any skin from the goat's cheese, then crumble it. Scatter over the bottom of the pastry case, followed by the basil leaves. Arrange the tomato halves in the case in two rings, leaving a space in the centre. **3.** Whisk together the cream and egg yolks in a jug with seasoning to taste. **4.** Place the tart tin on the pulled-out oven rack. Pour the egg and cream mix into the pastry case, right to the top. Carefully slide into the oven and bake for 25–35 minutes until set. **5.** Allow to cool on a wire rack before serving.

## BRITISH SALAD WITH SALAD CREAM

*Serves 1*

Many of us would have had a salad like this when we were children. Ours is a nod to those dreary salads, but vastly improved! You can use all of the vegetables suggested or just a combination of the ones you like.

- **1–2 EGGS**
- **BREAKFAST RADISHES, TRIMMED**
- **SPRING ONIONS, TRIMMED**
- **CHERRY TOMATOES**
- **CUCUMBER, CUT IN THICK SLICES**
- **BUTTERHEAD LETTUCE, SEPARATED INTO LEAVES**
- **GREEN BEANS, BLANCHED FOR 2 MINUTES, REFRESHED IN ICED WATER AND COOLED**
- **CARROTS, CUT INTO STICKS**
- **CELERY, CUT INTO STICKS**
- **COOKED BEETROOT, PEELED AND CUT IN WEDGES**
- **SALAD CREAM (P206)**

**1.** Bring a pan of water to the boil. Add the eggs and hard-boil for 7 minutes. Drain and cool under cold running water, then peel and cut in half. **2.** Arrange the eggs and vegetables on serving plates, keeping all the ingredients separate. Serve with a bowl of salad cream.

NOTE: For a more substantial salad, add some good-quality sliced ham or cheese.

## CORONATION CHICKEN

*Serves 6–8 as a light dish,*
*or 4–6 as a main course*

This dish was devised in honour of the
Queen's coronation in 1953. Our version
has a long list of ingredients, but it is easily
made and can be prepared well in advance.

### POACHED CHICKEN

**I CHICKEN, APPROX. 1.8KG**
**2–3CM PIECE FRESH ROOT GINGER,**
  **SLICED**
**1/2 LEMON, SLICED**
**1/2 ORANGE, SLICED**
**I LEEK, ROUGHLY CHOPPED**
**2 CELERY STICKS, ROUGHLY**
  **CHOPPED**
**I ONION, ROUGHLY CHOPPED**
**I BULB GARLIC, HALVED**
  **HORIZONTALLY**
**I STAR ANISE**
**10 BLACK PEPPERCORNS**
**SALT AND GROUND BLACK PEPPER**

### SAUCE

**1/2 SMALL ONION, DICED**
**2 GARLIC CLOVES, FINELY**
  **CHOPPED**
**I TBSP FINELY CHOPPED FRESH**
  **ROOT GINGER**
**40G BUTTER**
**I TBSP CURRY POWDER**
**40G PLAIN WHITE FLOUR**
**90ML DOUBLE CREAM**
**30G CURRANTS OR CHOPPED**
  **DRIED APRICOTS**
**300ML MAYONNAISE (P203)**
**100G MANGO CHUTNEY, PURÉED**
  **UNTIL SMOOTH**
**JUICE OF 1/2 LEMON**
**100G THICK GREEK YOGHURT**

### TO SERVE

**I COS LETTUCE**
**70G TOASTED FLAKED ALMONDS**

**1.** Season the inside of the chicken with
salt and pepper. Place it in a saucepan large
enough for it to fit in comfortably. Add
the rest of the poaching ingredients and
pour in 1–2 litres of water to cover. Put
the lid on the pan. Bring to the boil, then
reduce to a very gentle simmer. Cook for
1 hour. Remove from the heat and leave
the chicken in the liquid until cool enough
to handle. **2.** Remove the chicken and set
aside. Strain the poaching liquid into a
clean pan. Bring to the boil and reduce
to 300ml. Reserve this reduced stock.
**3.** Pull the skin from the chicken and
discard. Remove the meat, discarding
bones and gristle, and tear into thick strips.
Set aside in the fridge while you prepare
the sauce. **4.** Sweat the onion, garlic and
ginger in the butter on a medium heat for
5–10 minutes until soft. Add the curry
powder and cook for 1–2 minutes, stirring,
then mix in the flour to make a roux. Add
the reduced stock and bring to a simmer,
stirring constantly. Stir in the cream. Pass
through a fine sieve, then add the currants
and cool. **5.** Mix the curry sauce base with
the mayonnaise, chutney, lemon juice and
yoghurt until well blended. Add the cooked
chicken and mix well. Cover and chill.
**6.** Divide the salad leaves among the
plates, or use to line a large shallow bowl.
Top with the chicken and scatter over the
toasted almonds.

NOTES: The chicken can be poached and
mixed with the sauce the day before ·
This would work well as part of a picnic,
but take the washed Cos leaves and toasted
almonds separately.

## DEVILLED KIDNEYS ON TOAST

*Serves 4*

People hardly ever cook this kind of Victorian breakfast dish any more, although we find it is still a hit, particularly with our older customers. It could be described as a real man's dish, with strong spicy flavours.

- **500G LAMBS' KIDNEYS**
- **1 TSP PAPRIKA**
- **1/2 TSP CAYENNE PEPPER**
- **A FEW DASHES OF TABASCO SAUCE**
- **2 TSP DIJON MUSTARD**
- **2 TSP WORCESTERSHIRE SAUCE**
- **1 HEAPED TBSP TOMATO KETCHUP**
- **2 TSP OLIVE OIL**
- **50ML MADEIRA**
- **80ML DOUBLE CREAM**
- **1 TBSP CHOPPED FRESH PARSLEY**
- **SALT**
- **4 THICK SLICES BROWN BREAD, TOASTED, TO SERVE**

**1.** Cut the kidneys in half and remove the cores with a pair of scissors. **2.** Mix together the paprika, cayenne, Tabasco, mustard, Worcestershire sauce and ketchup in a bowl. Add the kidneys and toss to coat. Leave to marinate for 1 hour. **3.** Heat up a large non-stick frying pan and add the oil. Make sure the pan is very hot, then add the kidneys and marinade. Season with salt. Sauté for a minute on each side. **4.** Add the Madeira and cook for 2 minutes. Add the cream, bring to the boil and cook for a further 1 minute. **5.** Stir in the parsley and serve on toast.

NOTE: As a more luxurious option, use veal kidneys cut into 3cm pieces.

## SMOKED MACKEREL AND POTATO SALAD

*Serves 4*

Mackerel is inexpensive and, being an oily fish, it is good for your health. Two very good reasons to enjoy it in a simply made salad like this. Warming the mackerel softens the texture and brings out the rich flavour.

- **400G ROSEVALE POTATOES, OR SIMILAR WAXY POTATOES**
- **4 EGGS**
- **4 SMOKED MACKEREL FILLETS**
- **20G FRESH CHIVES, CUT INTO 1CM LENGTHS**
- **80G PICKLED SHALLOTS (P208)**
- **SALT**
- **ABOUT 2 TBSP MUSTARD DRESSING (P206)**

**1.** Preheat the oven to 175°C. Peel and dice the potatoes. Cook in boiling salted water for 5–10 minutes just until tender. Drain and cool. **2.** Bring a pan of water to the boil. Add the eggs and hard-boil for 9 minutes. Drain and immerse in cold water. When the eggs are cool, peel and grate them. **3.** Remove any pin bones from the mackerel and peel off the skin. Divide into four portions and break each portion into two or three pieces. Warm the mackerel in the oven for 5 minutes. **4.** Gently toss together the potatoes, eggs, chives, pickled shallots and dressing. Divide among the plates and put the mackerel on top.

NOTE: Smoked eel fillet is also good in the salad, to replace the mackerel.

## POTTED DUCK, PICCALILLI AND TOAST

*Serves 6*

Potting – preserving meat or fish in a pot sealed with a layer of fat – has a very long history in this country. Our potted duck has a deep savoury flavour and we think it makes a good communal bowl for sharing, with toast and home-made piccalilli.

**4 DUCK LEGS, PREFERABLY**
**GRESSINGHAM DUCK**
**1 TSP SALT**
**1 GARLIC BULB**
**15 FRESH SAGE LEAVES, CHOPPED**
**3 BAY LEAVES**
**100ML PALE ALE**
**2 TBSP MADEIRA**
**BIG PINCH OF GROUND MACE**
**BLACK PEPPER**

TO SERVE
**PICCALILLI (P210)**
**12 SLICES BROWN BREAD, TOASTED**

**1.** Preheat the oven to 110°C. Sprinkle the duck legs with the salt and place in a casserole dish with a close-fitting lid. **2.** Separate the garlic cloves. Bash them with the back of a knife to crush roughly, then peel them. Add to the duck together with the sage, bay leaves and ale. **3.** Cover and cook in the oven for 2–3 hours until the meat is tender and falling off the bone. **4.** Drain off and reserve all the cooking liquid. When the meat is cool enough to handle, remove the skin and bones and shred the meat with your fingers. Put it into a bowl. Squash the garlic cloves and add to the shredded meat. Discard the bay leaves. **5.** Add the Madeira, mace and lots of pepper to the duck meat. Reserve a few tablespoons of the duck fat to seal the surface; slowly beat the remaining fat and cooking juices into the meat until all is incorporated and it looks creamy. Check the seasoning. **6.** Pack into an earthenware dish. Pour the reserved duck fat over the surface, then chill. **7.** Remove from the fridge half an hour before eating, to allow the potted duck to soften slightly. Serve with piccalilli and toast.

NOTE: The potted duck can be kept in the fridge for up to a week.

## GLAMORGAN SAUSAGES WITH BEETROOT RELISH
*Serves 4–6*

Not really 'sausages' in the true meat sense, this Welsh cheese version is still surprisingly savoury. Really good too. Beetroot relish provides just the right contrasting sweet-sharpness.

**150G LEEKS**
**25G BUTTER**
**10 FRESH SAGE LEAVES, CHOPPED**
**200G CAERPHILLY CHEESE**
**150G BOILED POTATOES**
**FRESHLY GRATED NUTMEG**
**50G SOFT WHITE BREADCRUMBS**
**SALT AND BLACK PEPPER**

TO FINISH
**60G PLAIN WHITE FLOUR**
**2 EGGS, BEATEN**
**100G DRIED WHITE BREADCRUMBS**
**SUNFLOWER OIL FOR SHALLOW FRYING**

TO SERVE
**BEETROOT RELISH (P209)**

**1.** Remove the outer layer and about one-quarter of the dark green ends from the leeks. Cut in half lengthways and in half again, then cut across into 5mm pieces. Wash well under cold running water; drain. **2.** Melt the butter in a pan and sweat the leeks over a medium heat for 5 minutes or until soft, making sure they don't brown at all. Add the sage and season with salt and pepper. Drain in a sieve and cool. **3.** Remove any rind from the cheese, then crumble into a bowl. **4.** Break up the potatoes with your hands and mix with the cheese and leeks. Season with pepper and a few gratings of nutmeg. **5.** Mix in the soft breadcrumbs. Knead into a ball and chill in the fridge for 1 hour.
**6.** Divide into approximately 50g pieces and roll each into a sausage shape about 10cm long. Chill in the freezer for 10 minutes. **7.** Gently roll the sausages in flour to coat all over, then dip in egg and, finally, coat evenly in breadcrumbs. Roll them on a flat surface to achieve an even shape. Place on a tray and keep in the fridge until you want to cook them. **8.** Shallow fry for 3–4 minutes until golden brown on all sides. Drain on kitchen paper. Serve hot, with beetroot relish.

NOTES: Don't make the sausages too fat or they will not cook through • If the mix is a bit sticky to shape neatly, pop the sausages into the freezer for 15 minutes • To give a very firm coating, you can dip the sausages in egg and breadcrumbs a second time, for a double layer.

## CRAB, FENNEL AND WATERCRESS SALAD
*Serves 4*

As we all hail from the West Country, we think that crabs from Newlyn and Brixham are superior. Wherever your crabs come from, buy from a good fishmonger, and be sure the crab is fresh, not frozen, which is truly horrible.

**400G FRESH, HAND-PICKED CRAB MEAT (BROWN AND WHITE MEAT KEPT SEPARATE)**
**1 TBSP TOMATO KETCHUP**
**70G CRÈME FRAÎCHE**
**GRATED ZEST AND JUICE OF 1 LEMON**
**1 TSP MADE ENGLISH MUSTARD**
**GREEN TABASCO SAUCE**
**WORCESTERSHIRE SAUCE**
**1 FENNEL BULB, WITH LEAVES IF POSSIBLE, OR 1 BUNCH BABY FENNEL**
**1 SMALL RED ONION, CUT IN HALF AND THINLY SLICED**
**2 BUNCHES WATERCRESS, PICKED AND WASHED**
**2 TBSP OLIVE OIL**
**SALT AND BLACK PEPPER**

GARLIC TOASTS
**4 THIN SLICES BREAD**
**1 GARLIC CLOVE, HALVED**
**OLIVE OIL**

1. Preheat the oven to 150°C. Put the brown crab meat into a bowl and add the ketchup, crème fraîche, lemon zest, mustard, and Tabasco and Worcestershire sauces to taste. Mix together and refrigerate. 2. Check the white meat for any shell or cartilage, then refrigerate. 3. For the toasts, rub the bread with the garlic and drizzle with olive oil, then bake for 10–15 minutes until crisp and golden. 4. Peel the fennel, halve lengthways and remove the core. Pick and wash the fennel leaves and dry on kitchen paper. Thinly slice the fennel halves on a mandoline. Squeeze a little lemon juice over the slices to prevent discoloration. 5. Toss the fennel, red onion, watercress and fennel leaves with the rest of the lemon juice, the olive oil and salt and pepper to taste. Divide among four plates, or put into a large bowl. 6. Scatter over the white crab meat. 7. Place a dollop of brown crab meat on each of the slices of toast and serve alongside.

NOTES: Don't use frozen crab meat – it simply won't be good enough • If you don't have a mandoline, slice the fennel as thinly as you can with a sharp knife.

## VEGETABLE AND PEARL BARLEY SOUP
*Serves 4*

This chunky, filling soup needs nothing more than some good bread to make a satisfying meal. It was designed to appeal to vegans and vegetarians, but everyone loves it.

- **I MEDIUM ONION**
- **100G CELERY (ABOUT 4 STICKS), LEAVES RESERVED**
- **100G SWEDE**
- **100G CARROTS**
- **100G LEEKS**
- **25ML OLIVE OIL**
- **2 GARLIC CLOVES, CHOPPED**
- **A FEW SPRIGS OF FRESH THYME**
- **I LITRE VEGETABLE STOCK (SEE P202, NOTE)**
- **35G PEARL BARLEY**
- **HANDFUL OF SHREDDED SAVOY OR HISPI CABBAGE**
- **HANDFUL OF FRESH CURLY PARSLEY, STALKS DISCARDED**
- **SALT AND BLACK PEPPER**

1. Peel or trim the vegetables, then cut into 1cm dice. 2. Heat up the olive oil in a saucepan and sweat the onion, celery stalks, swede, carrots and leeks for about 15 minutes or until soft, without browning. Add the garlic and thyme and cook for a further 5 minutes. 3. Add the stock and salt to taste. Stir well. Bring to the boil and cook for 10 minutes. 4. Stir in the pearl barley and simmer gently for 20 minutes, stirring occasionally. 5. Add the shredded cabbage and the celery and parsley leaves. Bring back to the boil and simmer for 5 minutes. Season with lots of black pepper and serve hot.

NOTE: You could use Meat stock (p202) instead of vegetable, which will make a richer soup that is obviously no longer vegetarian.

## LEEK AND POTATO SOUP

*Serves 4*

Here's a comforting, simple-to-make soup for colder weather. It is similar to vichyssoise, although it is chunky, not smooth, and it doesn't need any cream to make it satisfying.

**500G LEEKS**
**4 TSP OLIVE OIL**
**50G BUTTER**
**1 MEDIUM ONION, DICED**
**500G POTATOES, PEELED AND CUT**
   **IN SMALL CHUNKS OR SLICES**
**600ML CHICKEN OR VEGETABLE**
   **STOCK (P202)**
**4 BAY LEAVES**
**400ML MILK**
**SALT AND BLACK PEPPER**
**SNIPPED FRESH CHIVES TO**
   **GARNISH**

1. Cut the leeks into four lengthways, then cut across into squares and wash thoroughly. 2. Heat up the oil and butter in a saucepan and sweat half of the leeks with the onion for about 10 minutes or until soft and translucent. 3. Add the potatoes and season with salt. Cook, uncovered, for 5 more minutes. 4. Add the stock and bay leaves. Bring to the boil, then simmer for about 15 minutes or until the potatoes start to fall apart. 5. Add the remaining leeks together with the milk. Season with salt and pepper. Bring back to the boil and simmer for 5 minutes. Sprinkle with chives and serve.

NOTE: If you want a smooth soup, remove the bay leaves before blending.

## CAULIFLOWER SOUP

*Serves 6*

A cauliflower soup may sound boring, but this one is really tasty. The slow cooking of the cauliflower and onions in butter first is the trick. The result is a beautifully pale and creamy soup.

**1 LARGE CAULIFLOWER,**
   **WEIGHING ABOUT 1KG**
**1 LARGE ONION, CHOPPED**
**60G BUTTER**
**500ML VEGETABLE STOCK**
   **(SEE P202, NOTE)**
**4 BAY LEAVES**
**250–400ML MILK**
**SALT AND WHITE PEPPER**

1. Remove the leaves from the cauliflower but not the stalks. Roughly chop the cauliflower. 2. Sweat the onion in the butter for about 10 minutes or until soft, ensuring it does not brown. 3. Add the cauliflower and some salt. Cover and cook for 10 minutes. 4. Pour in the stock and add the bay leaves. Bring to the boil, then cover again and simmer for 25–30 minutes until the cauliflower is tender. Discard the bay leaves. 5. Blend until smooth. Pour into a clean pan and add the milk. Stir well. Bring back to the boil. Check the seasoning and serve.

## PUMPKIN SOUP
*Serves 4–6*

Orange-fleshed pumpkins and squashes make the smoothest soups with a fabulous rich colour. But don't use a huge Halloween pumpkin, which has been grown for carving, not eating. It will be too watery and stringy.

**1–2KG PUMPKIN OR ORANGE-
    FLESHED SQUASH
1 MEDIUM ONION, SLICED
4 GARLIC CLOVES, PEELED
10 FRESH SAGE LEAVES
GRATED ZEST AND JUICE OF
    1 ORANGE
500ML VEGETABLE STOCK
    (SEE P202, NOTE)
SALT AND BLACK PEPPER**

**1.** Preheat the oven to 180°C. Remove the skin from the pumpkin. Cut into wedges and remove the seeds and fibres. **2.** Place the pumpkin wedges in an ovenproof dish with the onion, garlic, sage, and orange zest and juice. Cover with a lid and cook in the oven for 1½–2 hours until the pumpkin is very tender. **3.** Leave until cool enough to handle, then blend everything with the stock until smooth. Check the seasoning and reheat for serving.

## ROAST TOMATO SOUP
*Serves 4*

As long as your tomatoes are ripe, this soup will have a good rich colour. If you grow your own, it's a great way to use up a glut, particularly the squashy, overripe ones. The soup's flavour is nicely piquant due to a bit of vinegar and paprika.

**2KG RIPE TOMATOES
500ML PASSATA
50ML OLIVE OIL
25ML SHERRY VINEGAR
5 SPRIGS OF FRESH THYME
5 BAY LEAVES
3 GARLIC CLOVES, CRUSHED
1 TSP SMOKED PAPRIKA
SALT AND BLACK PEPPER**

**1.** Preheat the oven to 150°C. Cut the tomatoes in half and place in a deep casserole with a lid. Mix in all the other ingredients. **2.** Cover the casserole and cook in the oven for 2 hours, stirring after 1½ hours. **3.** Remove from the oven and pass the tomato mixture through a mouli (vegetable mill) or a fine sieve. **4.** Taste and check the seasoning. Reheat if necessary, then serve with granary bread and butter.

NOTES: Taste the soup. If the tomatoes were very sharp, you may want to stir in 1 tablespoon caster sugar • On a hot summer day, try this soup chilled.

## CURRIED PARSNIP SOUP
*Serves 4*

One of the best things we British learned when we used to rule the world was the use of heat in recipes. All of us at Canteen love curry and other spicy food, and this soup is a favourite with us as well as our customers.

**25ML SUNFLOWER OIL**
**500G PARSNIPS, CHOPPED**
**1 MEDIUM ONION, CHOPPED**
**100G CELERIAC, CHOPPED**
**100G LEEKS, CHOPPED**
**4 GARLIC CLOVES, CRUSHED**
**3CM PIECE FRESH ROOT GINGER, GRATED**
**1 TBSP CURRY POWDER**
**1/2 TSP GROUND TURMERIC**
**1/2 TSP FENNEL SEEDS**
**1/2 TSP CORIANDER SEEDS**
**1 LITRE VEGETABLE STOCK (SEE P202, NOTE)**
**1 BUNCH SPRING ONIONS, SHREDDED**
**JUICE OF 1 LEMON**
**SALT AND BLACK PEPPER**

1. Heat up the sunflower oil in a large saucepan. Add the parsnips, onion, celeriac and leeks and sweat for about 10 minutes or until soft but not brown. 2. Add the garlic, ginger and spices. Cook for 5 more minutes, stirring occasionally. 3. Add the stock and some salt and and bring to the boil. Add the spring onions and simmer for 30–40 minutes until all the vegetables are tender. 4. Blend until smooth. Add the lemon juice and check the seasoning. If the soup is too thick, add more stock or some water. Reheat before serving, if necessary.

## PEA AND HAM SOUP
*Serves 6–8*

The English tradition of boiled salt pork and pease pudding is the inspiration for this soup. It is hearty and warming, which is just what you need when you feel that damp wintry chill in your bones.

**1 LARGE ONION, ROUGHLY CHOPPED**
**150G CELERY (ABOUT 6 STICKS), INCLUDING LEAVES, CUT IN CHUNKS**
**150G LEEKS, CHOPPED**
**4 GARLIC CLOVES, CHOPPED**
**2 LITRES GAMMON STOCK (P84)**
**200G DRIED SPLIT PEAS**
**SMALL HANDFUL OF PARSLEY STALKS, IF YOU HAVE THEM**
**100G GAMMON TRIMMINGS**
**10G FRESH CHIVES, SNIPPED**
**BLACK PEPPER**

1. Put the onion, celery, leeks and garlic into a saucepan. Add the stock, split peas and parsley stalks. 2. Bring to the boil, then simmer for 1–1½ hours until the peas are soft. 3. Remove from the heat and allow to cool for 30 minutes. Blend until smooth, then pass through a fine sieve. 4. Chop the gammon trimmings. Stir into the soup with the chives. If it is too thick, add some water. Season with black pepper. Reheat and serve hot.

NOTES: You should not need to add any salt to this soup because the gammon stock will be salty • If you don't have any gammon stock, or gammon trimmings, you can make this soup with Chicken or Meat stock (p202) and add some chopped cooked ham.

CHAPTER 3

# MAINS

## SLOW-ROAST PORK BELLY WITH APPLES
*Serves 6–8*

Pork is a big Canteen meat, and pork belly is a menu favourite. Slow-cooking this naturally fatty cut renders a lot of its fat but the result is still quite rich. Sage, cider and baked apples cut through the richness beautifully.

**1 PIECE PORK BELLY, WEIGHING ABOUT 2.5KG (ON THE BONE)**
**1 TSP GROUND FENNEL**
**1 GARLIC BULB, SEPARATED INTO CLOVES**
**20G FRESH SAGE LEAVES**
**500ML DRY CIDER**
**SALT AND BLACK PEPPER**

BAKED APPLES
**6 COX APPLES**
**50G BUTTER**
**GROUND ALLSPICE**

1. Preheat the oven to 150°C. With a sharp knife, score the belly across the skin at 2cm intervals. Season the meaty side of the belly with the ground fennel, 1 teaspoon salt and some black pepper 2. Bash the unpeeled garlic cloves and place them in a metal roasting tin with the sage. Set the pork belly on top. Pour over the cider and sprinkle the surface of the belly with 1 teaspoon salt. 3. Cover with a lid or foil and roast for 2 hours. If the pan dries out too much during the roasting, add a small amount of water. 4. Remove from the oven. Turn the oven up to 200°C. 5. Drain off the liquid and reserve in a saucepan. Put the pork belly back in the oven, uncovered, and roast for a further 45 minutes to 1 hour until the skin is crisp. 6. Meanwhile, prepare the apples. Cut them in half and remove the cores. Butter a metal baking sheet and place the apples in it cut-side down. Dab a little butter on top of each and sprinkle with a little allspice. Put into the oven with the pork and bake for 15 minutes. 7. Transfer the pork belly to a carving board, placing it fat-side down. Slide a knife under the rib bones and cut them off, keeping the knife against the bone. Set aside the meat and bones in a warm place. 8. Skim off any fat from the cooking liquid, then bring to the boil. 9. Cut the pork into thick slices and serve with the baked apples, the cooking juices and the ribs.

NOTE: In step 5, if the skin doesn't become crisp enough, remove the pork from the oven, cut off the skin and put it back in the oven to continue cooking. Meanwhile, cover the pork and keep warm.

## GAMMON WITH POTATOES AND PARSLEY SAUCE

*Serves 6*

Here's a traditional dish you once found in every pie shop and cafe. It is well worth a revival. Make this when you have more time at the weekend, and you'll have leftovers for the week – stock for soup and meat for sandwiches and salads or to mix into scrambled eggs.

**I CURED FREE-RANGE GAMMON OR BACON JOINT, WEIGHING ABOUT I.5KG**
**2 MEDIUM ONIONS, ROUGHLY CHOPPED**
**100G CARROTS, ROUGHLY CHOPPED**
**200G LEEKS, ROUGHLY CHOPPED**
**2 CELERY STICKS, ROUGHLY CHOPPED**
**20 BLACK PEPPERCORNS**
**2 BAY LEAVES**

TO SERVE
**IKG FLOURY POTATOES**
**SALT**
**PARSLEY SAUCE (P205)**

1. Put the gammon joint in a pan big enough to hold it comfortably. Add the vegetables, peppercorns and bay leaves. Cover with cold water. Bring to the boil, then simmer on a very low heat for 1 hour. **2.** Remove from the heat, cover the pan and leave for 1 hour to complete the cooking. **3.** About halfway through this time, peel the potatoes and cut into quarters. Place in a saucepan, cover with cold water and add some salt. Bring to the boil, then simmer for 20–25 minutes until tender. Drain well. **4.** Remove the gammon joint from the liquid. Cut off the skin/rind but leave a nice layer of fat. Discard the skin. **5.** Cut the gammon into slices of the desired thickness. Serve with the potatoes and with parsley sauce poured over the top.

NOTE: Strain and reserve the stock to use for Pea and ham soup (p76), along with any leftover gammon. Before using, taste the stock – if it is very salty, mix it with some cold water.

## SAUSAGES, MASH AND ONION GRAVY

*Serves 4*

The ultimate nursery food, a childhood favourite for almost everyone. We tried to pare it back to its essentials, making it as good as we could – plain potatoey mash and proper gravy that isn't sweet and treacly, to serve with the meatiest, juiciest pork sausages. Ours are made to our own recipe by Richard Woodall in Cumbria.

**800G FLOURY POTATOES, SUCH AS MARIS PIPER**
**8–12 GOOD-QUALITY MEATY PORK SAUSAGES**
**150G BUTTER, MELTED**
**SALT**
**ONION GRAVY (P202)**

1. Preheat the oven to 200°C. Peel the potatoes and cut into slices about 1cm thick. Rinse in cold water, then place in a saucepan. Cover with water, add some salt and bring to the boil. Simmer for about 15 minutes or until tender. 2. Meanwhile, place the sausages in an oiled roasting tray. Cook in the oven for 20 minutes, turning the sausages over halfway through the cooking. 3. Drain the potatoes well, reserving some of the cooking liquid. Return them to the pan and mash with a hand masher. Whisk in the melted butter plus a little of the cooking water to achieve the mash texture you like. Check the seasoning. 4. Serve the sausages with the mash and onion gravy.

## MACARONI CHEESE
*Serves 4–6*

We've all had bad experiences of macaroni cheese at school, which shouldn't put us off this big comfort dish. Our goal was to make a really good macaroni cheese, using the very best cheese, and we think we've got it right. It's a very popular dish on our menu.

**1/2 ONION, FINELY DICED**
**800ML FULL-FAT MILK**
**60G BUTTER**
**60G PLAIN WHITE FLOUR**
**320G STRONG CHEDDAR, GRATED**
**400ML DOUBLE CREAM**
**1 TBSP DIJON MUSTARD**
**400G MACARONI**
**50G PARMESAN, FRESHLY GRATED**
**SALT AND BLACK PEPPER**

1. Preheat the oven to 180°C. Put the onion into a saucepan with the milk and bring to the boil. 2. In another, large saucepan, melt the butter. Add the flour and stir to mix, then cook over a medium heat for 2–3 minutes. 3. Slowly pour in the boiling milk, whisking constantly to ensure there are no lumps. Bring back to the boil, still whisking so that the sauce doesn't stick and burn. 4. Remove from the heat and beat in the Cheddar until melted. Stir in the cream and mustard. Set aside. 5. Add the macaroni to a pot of boiling salted water. Stir once to ensure the pasta does not stick together, then cook for exactly 4 minutes. Drain. 6. Pour the macaroni into the sauce. Season with black pepper and mix together. 7. Transfer to an ovenproof dish. Sprinkle with the grated Parmesan and bake for 25–35 minutes until bubbling and the top is golden.

NOTE: Try mixing in one of the following before baking: 200g skinless smoked haddock fillet, diced; 5–6 rashers dry-cure bacon, grilled and crumbled; or 250g spinach leaves, chopped.

# PIES

## SPICY MUTTON PIE
*Serves 6*

The rich filling for this pie was inspired by
our favourite East End Indian restaurants.
It's made with mutton, which has an
undeserved image today of being old
knackered meat. This just isn't true. It
is very tasty, and works really well with
the spices.

**2 TBSP SUNFLOWER OIL**
**I MEDIUM ONION, CUT IN ICM DICE**
**150G CARROTS, CUT IN ICM DICE**
**100G FENNEL, CUT IN ICM DICE**
**2 TSP CURRY POWDER**
**I TSP MUSTARD SEEDS**
**1/2 TSP CAYENNE PEPPER**
**I TSP GROUND GINGER**
**I TSP GROUND CORIANDER**
**4 GARLIC CLOVES, CHOPPED**
**IKG BONED LEG OF MUTTON, CUT**
    **IN 2–3CM DICE**
**400G CAN CHOPPED TOMATOES**
**30G TREACLE**
**250ML MEAT STOCK (P202)**
**I HEAPED TBSP TOMATO PURÉE**
**150G PEELED AND DICED**
    **POTATOES**
**SALT**

TO FINISH
**700G PUFF PASTRY**
**I EGG, BEATEN**

**1.** Heat up the oil in a large, heavy-
bottomed pan and sweat the onion,
carrots and fennel for about 15 minutes
or until soft but not brown. **2.** Add all the
spices and the garlic. Stir well. Cook for
5 minutes. **3.** Add the mutton together with
the tomatoes, treacle, stock, tomato purée
and some salt. Bring to the boil, then cover
and simmer gently for 2–3 hours, stirring
occasionally. **4.** Add the potatoes and cook
for a further 30 minutes or until the meat
is tender but not falling apart. Remove
from the heat and allow to cool completely.
**5.** Preheat the oven to 170°C. Butter the
inside of a 28–30cm oval pie dish that is at
least 8cm deep. **6.** Roll out the pastry on a
well-floured board to a thickness of 3mm.
Cut out an oval piece of pastry to line the
dish. The pastry needs to be long and wide
enough to cover the bottom and sides of
the dish, with some extra for overhang.
Place in the dish, leaving the edges hanging
over the sides. Brush the overhang with
a little beaten egg. **7.** Fill with the cold
pie filling. Cut a piece of pastry for the
lid – this should be slightly larger than
the dish – and lay it over the filling. Dip
your fingers in flour and pinch the edges
of the lid to the edges of the pastry lining
the dish, to seal them together. Trim off
excess pastry with a knife. **8.** Cut three or
four 1-cm slits in the lid, to allow steam
to escape during baking. Brush the lid
with beaten egg to glaze. Bake for 35–40
minutes until the pastry is golden brown
and the filling is bubbling around the edges
and through the slits in the lid. Serve hot.

NOTES: If you like your food quite spicy,
use a hot curry powder, or add more curry
powder to taste • As with all of the pie
fillings, this is delicious simply eaten on
its own as a stew • We serve our pies with
mash, gravy and greens, but they're just
as good with boiled potatoes and other
vegetables or with salad.

## STEAK AND KIDNEY PIE
*Serves 6*

Here's a great British classic that has retained its huge popularity over the years. We've kept it quite traditional, but made our pie the best one ever. When you cut through the buttery crust, it smells gorgeous.

**40G BEEF DRIPPING OR 3 TBSP OLIVE OIL**

**1 MEDIUM ONION, CUT IN 1CM DICE**

**150G CARROTS, CUT IN 1CM DICE**

**100G CELERY, CUT IN 1CM DICE**

**1KG BEEF CHUCK, CUT IN 2–3CM DICE**

**1 1/2 TBSP PLAIN WHITE FLOUR**

**250ML GUINNESS**

**250ML MEAT STOCK (P202)**

**2 TSP WORCESTERSHIRE SAUCE**

**100G LEEKS, DICED**

**2 GARLIC CLOVES, CHOPPED**

**10G FRESH THYME SPRIGS, TIED IN A BUNDLE**

**2 BAY LEAVES**

**500G OX KIDNEYS (PREPARED BY THE BUTCHER), DICED**

**SALT AND BLACK PEPPER**

TO FINISH

**700G PUFF PASTRY**

**1 EGG, BEATEN**

**1.** Heat up half of the dripping or oil in a metal casserole until hot and lightly smoking. Add the onion, carrots and celery and sauté for 5–10 minutes to brown lightly. Remove from the pan. **2.** Season the beef with salt and pepper. Get the pan very hot and add more of the dripping or oil if there is none left from the vegetables. Brown off the meat for 5 minutes (do this in batches), turning the dice to ensure they are well coloured on all sides. **3.** When all the beef is browned and back in the casserole, sprinkle over the flour and stir well. Add the Guinness, stock and Worcestershire sauce, scraping any tasty residue from the bottom of the pan and mixing it into the liquid. **4.** Add the sautéed vegetables, leeks, garlic, thyme and bay leaves. Cover and cook over a very low heat for 1 hour. **5.** Season the diced kidneys. Add to the pan and cook, covered, for a further 1–1½ hours until all the meat is tender. **6.** Remove from the heat and check the seasoning. Allow to cool completely. **7.** Assemble and bake the pie (see Spicy mutton pie, p90, steps 5–8). Serve hot.

NOTE: Oysters used to be common in steak and kidney pie, and adding a drained can of smoked oysters will give an old-fashioned flavour here. Stir into the cooled filling before assembling the pie.

## CHICKEN AND MUSHROOM PIE
*Serves 6*

A pie like this would once have been a regular midweek meal at home, and you wouldn't see it on restaurant menus. On our menu, though, it is a perennial hit. The filling is flavoursome and rich, with a little touch of dried porcini giving a really deep savouriness.

2 TSP OLIVE OIL
45G BUTTER
I MEDIUM ONION, DICED
100G CELERY, DICED
200G LEEKS, DICED
2 GARLIC CLOVES, CHOPPED
10G FRESH TARRAGON SPRIGS,
 LEAVES PICKED AND CHOPPED
700G SKINLESS CHICKEN THIGH
 MEAT, CUT IN 4–5CM CHUNKS
I HEAPED TBSP DRIED PORCINI
300ML CHICKEN STOCK (P202)
100ML WHITE WINE
25G PLAIN WHITE FLOUR
200ML DOUBLE CREAM
I HEAPED TBSP DIJON MUSTARD
200G BUTTON MUSHROOMS,
 HALVED
SALT AND WHITE PEPPER

TO FINISH
700G PUFF PASTRY
I EGG, BEATEN

1. Heat the oil and 25g of the butter in a large, heavy-bottomed pan. Sweat the onion, celery and half the leeks for about 10 minutes or until soft and translucent.
2. Add the garlic, tarragon, chicken, dried porcini, stock, wine and ½ teaspoon salt. Cover and cook on a low heat for 30–45 minutes until the chicken is cooked through. 3. Pour into a sieve set over a bowl, to strain the cooking liquid. Reserve the chicken mixture. 4. Melt the remaining 20g butter in a clean pan. Whisk in the flour and cook for 2–3 minutes until bubbling. Gradually whisk in the cooking liquid and bring to a simmer. Whisk in the cream and mustard and check the seasoning. Remove from the heat.
5. Add the chicken mixture, mushrooms and remaining leeks to the sauce and mix together. Allow to cool completely.
6. Assemble and bake the pie (see Spicy mutton pie, p90, steps 5–8). Serve hot.

## DUCK, CHESTNUT AND PRUNE PIE

*Serves 6*

The spices, fruit, nuts and game of Elizabethan England inspired this pie and give it a Christmassy feel. We may be a bit bah-humbug about Christmas, but at that time of year we have this, or a turkey pie, on the menu. It is very, very good, and also great served cold.

**3 TBSP OLIVE OIL**
**I MEDIUM ONION, DICED**
**100G CARROTS, DICED**
**100G CELERY, DICED**
**100G CELERIAC, DICED**
**4 GARLIC CLOVES, FINELY**
    **CHOPPED**
**250ML PALE ALE**
**250ML MEAT STOCK (P202)**
**20 FRESH SAGE LEAVES, CHOPPED**
**BIG PINCH OF GROUND MACE**
**BIG PINCH OF GROUND ALLSPICE**
**500G SKINLESS DUCK LEG MEAT,**
    **CUT IN CHUNKS**
**200G LEEKS, DICED**
**80G PEELED COOKED CHESTNUTS,**
    **CHOPPED**
**50G STONED PRUNES, CHOPPED**
**2 TBSP CORNFLOUR**
**SALT AND BLACK PEPPER**

TO FINISH
**700G PUFF PASTRY**
**I EGG, BEATEN**

**I.** Heat up the oil in a big saucepan. Add the onion, carrots, celery and celeriac and sweat for 10–15 minutes until soft. **2.** Add the garlic, ale, stock, sage, mace, allspice and duck leg meat plus some salt and pepper. Cover and cook on a low heat for 1–1½ hours until the meat is very tender. **3.** Add the leeks, chestnuts and prunes. Cook for 2 minutes. **4.** Mix the cornflour with a little water, then add to the pan. Cook, stirring, until thickened. Check the seasoning. Allow to cool completely. **5.** Assemble and bake the pie (see Spicy mutton pie, p90, steps 5–8). Serve hot.

## RABBIT AND BACON PIE
*Serves 6*

To some people, rabbit is scary and they won't even try cooking it. But just think of a rabbit as a speedier chicken and have a go. If the rabbit is wild it will have more flavour than a farmed bunny, although either is fine in this pie.

POACHED RABBIT

**I RABBIT, PREFERABLY WILD**
**I MEDIUM ONION, DICED**
**IOOG CELERIAC, DICED**
**IOOG CARROTS, DICED**
**4 GARLIC CLOVES, CRUSHED**
**I SPRIG OF FRESH SAGE**
**I SPRIG OF FRESH ROSEMARY**
**I SPRIG OF FRESH THYME**
**2 BAY LEAVES**
**200ML MEAT STOCK (P202)**
**200ML CIDER**
**SALT AND BLACK PEPPER**

PIE FILLING

**20G BUTTER**
**IOOG DRY-CURE STREAKY BACON**
**I50G LEEKS, DICED**
**I5G PLAIN WHITE FLOUR**
**20G FRESH CURLY PARSLEY,**
**   CHOPPED**

TO FINISH

**700G PUFF PASTRY**
**I EGG, BEATEN**

**1.** Preheat the oven to 150°C. Season the rabbit inside and out, then place in a casserole. **2.** Add all the other poaching ingredients with some salt and pepper. Cover and cook in the oven for 1 hour. **3.** Lift out the rabbit and set aside. Pour the liquid and vegetables into a sieve set over a bowl to strain the liquid. Discard the herb stalks. Reserve the liquid and vegetables separately. **4.** Pick the meat from the rabbit, discarding all skin and bones. Cut the meat into chunks. **5.** Melt the butter in a saucepan and fry the bacon for 4–5 minutes until lightly browned. **6.** Add the leeks and sweat for about 5 minutes or until soft. Add the flour and cook for 2 minutes, stirring. **7.** Add the reserved cooking liquid, mixing in well, then add the reserved poaching vegetables and rabbit meat. Bring to the boil and simmer for 5 minutes. **8.** Add the parsley, stir and remove from the heat. Check the seasoning. Allow to cool completely. **9.** Assemble and bake the pie (see Spicy mutton pie, p90, steps 5–8). Serve hot.

## FENNEL, TOMATO AND BASIL PIE
*Serves 6*

You may not think a savoury pie is a summer dish. This light, very aromatic vegetable pie will change your mind. It's great with some new potatoes and salad.

**3 TBSP OLIVE OIL**
**250G RED ONIONS, CUT IN**
**    1CM DICE**
**250G FENNEL, CUT IN 1CM DICE**
**4 GARLIC CLOVES, CHOPPED**
**1 TBSP CAPERS, CHOPPED**
**300ML PASSATA**
**250G COURGETTES, QUARTERED**
**    LENGTHWAYS, THEN CUT IN 2CM**
**    CHUNKS**
**250G TOMATOES, CUT IN CHUNKS**
**20G FRESH BASIL, LEAVES TORN**
**SALT AND BLACK PEPPER**

TO FINISH
**700G PUFF PASTRY**
**1 EGG, BEATEN**

1. Heat up 2 tablespoons of the oil in a frying pan and sweat the onions and fennel for about 5 minutes or until soft. Add the garlic and capers and cook for a further 5 minutes. **2.** Add the passata and some salt and stir well. Cover and cook over a low heat for 20 minutes. **3.** Meanwhile, heat the remainder of the oil in a saucepan until smoking. Add the courgettes and cook for 3–4 minutes until they are browning slightly. Remove from the pan and put to one side. **4.** When the tomato sauce is ready, mix in the cooked courgettes, the tomatoes and basil. Season to taste. Allow to cool completely. **5.** Assemble and bake the pie (see Spicy mutton pie, p90, steps 5–8). Serve hot.

NOTE: For a spicier mix, add ½ teaspoon dried chilli flakes with the garlic.

## WILD MUSHROOM PIE
*Serves 6*

If you're lucky enough to forage for your own wild mushrooms, there's a great native variety waiting. Any edible wild mushroom can be used for this pie – just cut huge ones into bite-size pieces.

**4 TBSP OLIVE OIL**
**35G BUTTER**
**I MEDIUM ONION, DICED**
**100G LEEKS, DICED**
**10G FRESH THYME, LEAVES PICKED**
**    AND CHOPPED**
**15G DRIED PORCINI, CHOPPED**
**75ML WHITE WINE**
**300ML DOUBLE CREAM**
**500G MIXED CULTIVATED**
**    MUSHROOMS, HALVED OR**
**    QUARTERED ACCORDING**
**    TO SIZE**
**200G MIXED WILD MUSHROOMS**
**2 GARLIC CLOVES, CHOPPED**
**15G FRESH PARSLEY, CHOPPED**
**SALT AND BLACK PEPPER**

TO FINISH
**700G PUFF PASTRY**
**I EGG, BEATEN**

1. Heat up 2 tablespoons of the oil and the butter in a saucepan and sweat the onions and leeks for about 10 minutes or until soft. 2. Add the thyme, dried porcini and wine. Simmer for 5–10 minutes until the wine has evaporated. Stir in the cream and cook for a further 5 minutes. Remove from the heat. 3. Fry off the mushrooms with the garlic in two batches, using half of the remaining oil each time, in a hot frying pan for 3–4 minutes until the mushrooms are lightly browned. 4. Add the mushrooms with any juices to the other pan. Stir in the parsley and season to taste. Allow to cool completely. 5. Assemble and bake the pie (see Spicy mutton pie, p90, steps 5–8). Serve hot.

## SQUASH, CHARD AND SAGE PIE
*Serves 6*

Chard is a vegetable you see a lot in farmer's markets and it's usually included in organic veg box schemes, but most people don't know what to do with it. A hearty green with an earthy flavour, it goes well with sweet squash to make a pie for autumn.

**400G BUTTERNUT SQUASH**
**3 1/2 TBSP OLIVE OIL**
**1KG GREEN SWISS CHARD**
**25G BUTTER**
**1 MEDIUM ONION, DICED**
**100G CELERY, DICED**
**100G LEEKS, DICED**
**15 FRESH SAGE LEAVES**
**2 GARLIC CLOVES, CHOPPED**
**30G PLAIN WHITE FLOUR**
**350ML MILK**
**SALT AND BLACK PEPPER**

TO FINISH
**700G PUFF PASTRY**
**1 EGG, BEATEN**

**1.** Preheat the oven to 175°C. Peel the butternut squash and cut into 1-cm cubes. Toss with 2 tablespoons of the olive oil in a baking sheet, then roast for 15–20 minutes until tender. **2.** Meanwhile, separate the chard leaves and stalks. Dice the stalks and leaves, keeping them separate. **3.** Heat up the butter and remaining oil a saucepan and sweat the onion, celery and leeks on a low heat for 10–15 minutes until soft. Add the chard stalks, sage and garlic and cook for a further 5 minutes. **4.** Sprinkle over the flour and stir in well. Cook for 2–3 minutes until bubbling. Gradually stir in the milk and bring to the boil, stirring constantly. Remove from the heat. **5.** Mix together the vegetable sauce, butternut squash and chard leaves. Season with plenty of salt and pepper. Allow to cool completely. **6.** Assemble and bake the pie (see Spicy mutton pie, p90, steps 5–8). Serve hot.

## SHALLOT, THYME AND
## CHEDDAR PIE
*Serves 6*

Here, we took the traditional pasty filling
of cheese and onion to make a pie that is
genuinely very satisfying. You might feel a
little bit naughty when you eat it because it
is really rich!

**80G BUTTER**
**750G SHALLOTS, CUT INTO**
    **SIMILAR SIZES**
**350G CELERIAC, CUT IN 2CM**
    **CHUNKS**
**I GARLIC CLOVE, CHOPPED**
**20G FRESH THYME, LEAVES PICKED**
    **AND CHOPPED**
**250ML MILK**
**30G PLAIN WHITE FLOUR**
**200G STRONG CHEDDAR CHEESE,**
    **GRATED**
**200ML DOUBLE CREAM**
**2 TSP WHOLEGRAIN MUSTARD**
**SALT AND BLACK PEPPER**

TO FINISH
**700G PUFF PASTRY**
**I EGG, BEATEN**

**1.** Melt the butter in a saucepan and
sweat the shallots and celeriac over a
medium heat for about 15 minutes or
until softening. Add the garlic and thyme
and season to taste. Turn the heat down
low and cover the pan. Cook for about 5
minutes or until the vegetables are tender
but not browned. **2.** Heat up the milk in
another pan. **3.** Sprinkle the flour over
the vegetables and cook for 2–3 minutes,
stirring well. Gradually add the hot milk,
stirring, and bring to the boil. Cook
for about 5 minutes or until thickened.
Remove from the heat. **4.** Stir in the
cheese, double cream and mustard. Allow
to cool completely. **5.** Assemble and bake
the pie (see Spicy mutton pie, p90, steps
5–8). Serve hot.

# STEWS

## BEEF STEW WITH DUMPLINGS
*Serves 4*

This dish of Olde England is incredibly popular. It's made with an economical cut of beef that needs long, slow cooking to make it tender, and finished with old-fashioned suet dumplings. Makes your mouth water just to think of it.

**2 TBSP BEEF DRIPPING OR
    OLIVE OIL
2 MEDIUM ONIONS, CUT IN
    1CM DICE
100G CELERY, CUT IN 1CM DICE
150G CARROTS, CUT IN 1CM DICE
500G BONED SHIN OF BEEF, CUT IN
    3CM DICE
20G PLAIN WHITE FLOUR
250ML RED WINE
2 GARLIC CLOVES, CHOPPED
10G FRESH THYME SPRIGS, TIED IN
    A BUNDLE
4 BAY LEAVES
1 LITRE MEAT STOCK (P202)
SALT AND BLACK PEPPER**

SUET DUMPLINGS
**150G SELF-RAISING WHITE FLOUR
50G SUET
BIG PINCH OF SALT**

1. Preheat the oven to 135°C. Heat up the dripping or oil in a heavy pan with a lid until very hot. Add the onions, celery and carrots and sauté for 5–8 minutes to brown. Remove from the pan and keep to one side. 2. Season the meat. Put into the hot pan and brown off for 5 minutes, turning the dice to ensure all sides are well coloured. To brown the meat without stewing, the dice should be in a single layer in the pan, so if necessary brown in two batches. 3. Sprinkle the meat with the flour and stir through. Add the red wine and bring to the boil, stirring well.
4. Add the garlic, herbs and stock together with the browned vegetables. Cover the pan and bring back to the boil. 5. Place the covered pan in the oven and cook for 2–3 hours until the meat is tender.
6. Meanwhile, in a bowl mix together the ingredients for the dumplings, with 75ml water to bind. Shape into 12–15 walnut-sized balls. 7. When the beef is tender, check the seasoning of the stew, then place the dumplings on top. Cover the pan again and put back in the oven to cook for a further 25 minutes.

## LANCASHIRE HOTPOT

*Serves 6*

Few ingredients are needed to make this flavoursome potato-topped stew. Although lamb is normally used today, we make our hotpot with mutton, which was common up until the Second World War. We think the stronger mutton flavour works best.

**50G BUTTER**
**250G ONIONS, SLICED**
**1KG BONED LEG OF MUTTON, CUT**
   **IN 3–4CM DICE**
**150G CARROTS, SLICED**
**10G FRESH THYME, LEAVES PICKED**
**3 BAY LEAVES**
**700G FLOURY POTATOES, SUCH**
   **AS MARIS PIPER, PEELED AND**
   **THINLY SLICED**
**500ML MEAT STOCK (P202)**
**100ML PALE ALE**
**SALT AND BLACK PEPPER**

**1.** Preheat the oven to 135°C. Heat up half of the butter in a saucepan, add the onions and sweat over a low heat for about 15 minutes or until soft and translucent but not browned. **2.** Place the meat in an ovenproof dish and add the onions, carrots, thyme and bay leaves. Season well with salt and pepper and mix together. **3.** Arrange the potato slices on top of the meat and vegetable mix, overlapping the slices slightly. Melt the remaining butter and brush over the potatoes. Season with salt. **4.** Pour the stock and ale into the dish, then cover it. Cook in the oven for 2 hours. **5.** Remove the cover from the dish and increase the oven temperature to 150°C. Continue cooking for 30–45 minutes until the potato top is browned.

NOTE: You can also make this hotpot with neck of lamb instead of mutton. Reduce the cooking time in step 4 to 1½ hours.

## MUSHROOM, PEARL BARLEY AND CHARD STEW
*Serves 6*

Our aim with this stew was to create a satisfying main-course vegetarian dish without any cheese in it. We think we succeeded with this interesting combination of ingredients, including pearl barley rather than potatoes for a filling carb.

**IKG SWISS CHARD**
**4 TBSP OLIVE OIL**
**100G CELERIAC, CUT IN 2CM DICE**
**100G SWEDE, CUT IN 2CM DICE**
**100G TURNIP, CUT IN 2CM DICE**
**1 MEDIUM ONION, CUT IN 2CM DICE**
**4 GARLIC CLOVES, CHOPPED**
**1 LITRE VEGETABLE STOCK**
  **(SEE P202, NOTE)**
**50G PEARL BARLEY**
**1 HEAPED TBSP DRIED PORCINI**
**10G FRESH THYME SPRIGS**
**250G MIXED MUSHROOMS,**
  **QUARTERED**
**100G LEEK, CUT IN 1CM DICE**
**SALT AND BLACK PEPPER**

1. Separate the chard leaves from the stalks. Shred the leaves and chop the stalks.
2. Heat up 2 tablespoons of the olive oil in a large sauté pan and sweat the celeriac, swede, turnip and onion for 10–15 minutes until softening but not brown. 3. Add half of the garlic and the chard stalks and cook for a further 5 minutes, stirring. Season with salt and pepper. 4. Add the stock, pearl barley, porcini and thyme to the vegetables. Bring to the boil, then simmer for 20 minutes, stirring occasionally.
5. Meanwhile, heat up the remaining 2 tablespoons of oil in a frying pan until very hot. Add the remaining garlic with the mushrooms and fry for 3–4 minutes until lightly cooked. 6. Add the mushrooms, leek and chard leaves to the vegetable and barley stew and stir to mix. Bring back to the boil. Check the seasoning before serving.

## RED PEPPER, GREEN BEAN AND CAPER STEW

*Serves 4*

Big on flavour and a little bit spicy, this stew really delivers. Blackening the peppers provides a good smoky background taste, which is heightened by a kick of hot smoked paprika.

250G RED PEPPERS
3 TBSP OLIVE OIL
200G RED ONIONS, CUT IN
  WEDGES
4 TSP SHERRY VINEGAR
100G GREEN BOBBY BEANS,
  HALVED
1 TBSP CAPERS
2 GARLIC CLOVES, CHOPPED
1/2 TSP HOT SMOKED PAPRIKA
250G PASSATA
100ML VEGETABLE STOCK
  (SEE P202, NOTE)
SALT AND BLACK PEPPER

1. Quarter the red peppers lengthways and remove the pith and seeds. Cut each quarter into three triangular pieces.
2. Heat up a splash of the olive oil in a large frying pan until very hot. Sear the peppers and onions in small batches for 4–5 minutes or until slightly blackened, finishing off each batch with a few splashes of sherry vinegar. Add more oil to the pan for each batch. 3. Transfer the peppers and onions to a large saucepan and add the green beans, capers, garlic, smoked paprika, passata and stock. Bring to the boil, then cover and simmer for 30 minutes, stirring occasionally. Season to taste before serving.

NOTE: Don't be shy about blackening the edges of the peppers. This is what gives the smoky flavour to the stew.

## BROAD BEAN, POTATO, SPINACH AND MINT STEW
*Serves 4*

People don't use broad beans much, probably because they are fiddly to prepare with all that podding and skinning (if they're small and tender you don't have to remove the skins). But we love them because of their texture and nice flavour, wonderful in this summer stew.

**250G FROZEN SHELLED BROAD BEANS, THAWED**
**200G NEW POTATOES, LIGHTLY RUMBLED (SCRAPED)**
**2 TBSP OLIVE OIL**
**I MEDIUM ONION, SLICED**
**2 GARLIC CLOVES, CHOPPED**
**I LITRE VEGETABLE STOCK (SEE P202, NOTE)**
**250G SPINACH, CHOPPED**
**IOG FRESH MINT, CHOPPED**
**SALT AND BLACK PEPPER**

1. Slip the broad beans out of their tough skins. 2. Cut the potatoes in half lengthways, then slice across into four. 3. Heat up the olive oil a large saucepan and sweat the potatoes with the onion for about 10 minutes or until softening, without allowing the vegetables to brown. Add the garlic and cook for a further minute. 4. Add the stock and some salt. Bring to the boil, then cover and simmer for about 10 minutes or until the potatoes are tender. 5. Add the broad beans and cook for a further 5 minutes. 6. Add the chopped spinach and stir in. Cook for 2–3 minutes until wilted. 7. Mix in the mint and season with pepper to taste.

## WINTER ROOT VEGETABLE STEW WITH CHEDDAR DUMPLINGS

*Serves 4*

Root vegetables are a British winter staple. Some people are prejudiced against them (those school dinners have a lot to answer for!), but they make a hearty stew that is far from boring. We top it with light, fluffy dumplings that are reminiscent of a cheese scone.

**I MEDIUM ONION**
**IOOG TURNIPS**
**150G SWEDE**
**150G CELERIAC**
**200G LEEKS**
**25ML OLIVE OIL**
**25G BUTTER**
**3 GARLIC CLOVES, CHOPPED**
**15 FRESH SAGE LEAVES, CHOPPED**
**3 BAY LEAVES**
**750ML VEGETABLE STOCK**
   **(SEE P202, NOTE)**
**CHOPPED FRESH PARSLEY AND**
   **CHIVES TO GARNISH**

DUMPLINGS
**20G BUTTER**
**IOOG SELF-RAISING WHITE FLOUR**
**50G CHEDDAR CHEESE, GRATED**
**1/2 TSP ENGLISH MUSTARD POWDER**
**BIG PINCH OF SALT**
**ABOUT 2 TBSP MILK**

**1.** Peel or trim all the vegetables, then cut into 2-cm dice. **2.** Heat up the oil and butter in a large saucepan. Add the onion, turnips, swede and celeriac and sweat for 10–15 minutes on a medium heat until softening, ensuring the vegetables do not brown. **3.** Add the garlic and cook for 5 more minutes. **4.** Add the leeks, sage, bay leaves and vegetable stock. Bring to the boil, then cover the pan. Simmer for 20 minutes. **5.** Meanwhile, make the dumplings. Rub the butter into the flour until the mixture is like crumbs. Mix in the cheese, mustard and salt. Gently mix in enough milk to bind to a firm dough. Shape into walnut-sized balls. **6.** Preheat the oven to 175°C. **7.** Check the seasoning of the vegetable stew, then place the dumplings on the surface. Place in the oven. Cook, uncovered, for 15–20 minutes until the dumplings are puffed and lightly browned. **8.** Sprinkle with chopped parsley and chives to serve.

## CAWL
*Serves 6*

Traditionally Welsh, this brothy stew of lamb and vegetables is amazingly good and a meal in itself. You can add more vegetables, such as swede and turnip, if you like. In Wales it is often served with a slice of Caerphilly cheese.

**2KG LAMB SHOULDER (ON THE BONE), CUT IN HALF BY THE BUTCHER**
**100G CELERY, ROUGHLY CHOPPED**
**100G CARROTS, ROUGHLY CHOPPED**
**1 ONION, ROUGHLY CHOPPED**
**300G LEEKS, TRIMMED (TRIMMINGS RESERVED AND ROUGHLY CHOPPED) AND CUT IN 2–3CM THICK PIECES**
**1 GARLIC BULB, CUT IN HALF HORIZONTALLY**
**A LARGE SPRIG EACH OF FRESH THYME, PARSLEY AND ROSEMARY**
**6 BAY LEAVES**
**300G FLOURY POTATOES, PEELED AND CUT IN 3CM CHUNKS**
**SALT AND BLACK PEPPER**

**1.** Preheat the oven to 150°C. Season the lamb well and place in a deep ovenproof pan. Mix in the roughly chopped celery, carrots, onion and leek trimmings, the halved head of garlic and the herbs. Add 2 litres of water. **2.** Cover the pan and cook in the oven for 2–3 hours until the lamb is tender. **3.** Drain off the stock and set aside to cool. Discard the chopped vegetables, garlic and herb stalks. Reserve the bay leaves. **4.** When the lamb is cool enough to handle, remove the meat and cut into large chunks. Discard the fat and bones. **5.** Skim off the fat from the lamb stock. Reserve 2–3 tablespoons fat and discard the rest. **6.** Heat up the reserved lamb fat in a large saucepan and cook the potatoes, seasoning with salt and pepper, on a low heat for 10–15 minutes until tender. **7.** Add the reserved lamb stock and bay leaves and bring to the boil. Simmer for 10 minutes. Add the leek pieces and simmer for 5 more minutes. Season with lots of black pepper. **8.** Add the chunks of lamb and simmer for a further 5 minutes before serving.

## VENISON AND ALE STEW
*Serves 4*

Venison is a healthy lean meat with a
good taste, fine-grained and not fibrous.
It becomes fabulously tender in this stew,
which is aromatic with spices and ale.
A good winter dish, the stew needs mash
or boiled potatoes with it so you can enjoy
every bit of the gravy.

2 TBSP OLIVE OIL
I MEDIUM ONION, CUT IN ICM DICE
100G CARROTS, CUT IN ICM DICE
200G CELERIAC, CUT IN ICM DICE
500G BONED HAUNCH OF
      VENISON, CUT IN 2–3CM DICE
20G PLAIN WHITE FLOUR
200ML PALE ALE
1/2 TSP GROUND ALLSPICE
BIG PINCH OF GROUND MACE
BIG PINCH OF GROUND GINGER
2 TSP TOMATO PURÉE
I GARLIC CLOVE, CHOPPED
3 SPRIGS OF FRESH THYME
3 SPRIGS OF FRESH ROSEMARY
2 BAY LEAVES
GRATED ZEST OF I ORANGE
500ML MEAT STOCK (P202)
SALT AND BLACK PEPPER

**1.** Heat up the oil in a heavy saucepan until
hot. Add the onion, carrots and celeriac
and sauté for 5–8 minutes to brown.
Remove from the pan and keep to one side.
**2.** Season the meat, then place in the hot
pan and brown off for 5 minutes, turning
the dice so all sides are well coloured.
To brown the meat without stewing, the
dice should be in a single layer in the pan,
so if necessary brown in two batches.
**3.** Sprinkle the meat with the flour and stir
through. Add the pale ale, allspice, mace,
ginger and tomato purée and stir to mix.
Bring to the boil, stirring occasionally.
**4.** Add the garlic, herbs, orange zest
and stock together with the browned
vegetables. Bring back to the boil, then
cover the pan. Reduce the heat to low and
simmer for 2–3 hours until the meat is
tender. Check the seasoning before serving.

NOTES: We use pale ale made by Meantime,
a microbrewery in Greenwich • If it's more
convenient, you can cook the stew in a
150°C oven for the same time.

# ROASTS AND GRILLS

## ROAST DUCK LEGS
*Serves 4*

This is like confit duck because the legs are roasted immersed in fat. To achieve this it's important to use a dish that will hold the duck legs close. The result is very moist and aromatic. Nice with braised red cabbage (see the recipe on p134).

**8 WHOLE DUCK LEGS, PREFERABLY GRESSINGHAM DUCK**
**1/2 TSP FENNEL SEEDS**
**I ORANGE, QUARTERED AND SQUEEZED**
**A FEW SPRIGS OF FRESH THYME**
**I GARLIC BULB, SEPARATED INTO CLOVES AND BASHED**
**SALT AND BLACK PEPPER**

GRAVY
**I TBSP PLAIN WHITE FLOUR**
**1/2 GLASS WHITE WINE OR CIDER**
**500ML MEAT STOCK (P202)**

TO SERVE
**ROAST POTATOES (P130)**
**APPLE SAUCE (P136)**

1. Preheat the oven to 150°C. Toss the duck legs with the fennel, salt and pepper. Squeeze over the orange juice, then place the orange skins in a flameproof ovenproof dish that will hold the duck legs snugly. Add the thyme and garlic. Arrange the duck legs, skin-side up, in the dish.
2. Roast for about 1½ hours or until the duck legs are cooked. To test, press one with your finger – the meat should not give any resistance. 3. Pour off the fat and juices from the dish through a strainer into a bowl. Leave to settle. Lift the duck legs on to a warm serving dish and set aside while you make the gravy. 4. Remove the fat from the cooking juices (reserve the fat for later use). Return the juices to the ovenproof dish with the garlic and herbs. (Discard the orange skins.) 5. Sprinkle the flour into the dish and place on the heat. Stir the flour into the roasting juices, scraping the bottom well to remove any residue. Add the wine and bubble for a few minutes, then add the stock and whisk in well. Strain into a saucepan. Bring to the boil, then simmer for a few minutes. Check the seasoning. 6. Serve the duck legs with the gravy, plus roast potatoes, some vegetables and apple sauce.

NOTE: Keep the duck fat for roasting potatoes.

## ROAST RIB OF BEEF
*Serves 6–8*

The classic British Sunday lunch of a big roast joint of beef with all the trimmings cannot be bettered. Choose well-hung beef with good marbling, and season it with plenty of salt before cooking, so that it will have a really savoury crisp crust. If you have leftovers, make sandwiches – we use leftover Yorkshire puds instead of bread, and add some watercress and horseradish sauce, too.

**I BONED AND ROLLED RIB OF BEEF (ON THE BONE), WEIGHING ABOUT 2KG**
**SALT AND BLACK PEPPER**

GRAVY
**I TBSP PLAIN WHITE FLOUR**
**1/2 GLASS RED WINE**
**500ML MEAT STOCK (P202)**

TO SERVE
**ROAST POTATOES (P130)**
**YORKSHIRE PUDDING (P130)**
**HORSERADISH SAUCE (P137)**

**I.** Remove the meat from the fridge at least an hour before you intend to cook it. Preheat the oven to 225°C. **2.** Season the meat well with salt and black pepper, then place in a roasting tray. Roast for about 30 minutes or until well browned. **3.** Reduce the heat to 130°C and continue roasting for 20 minutes for a rare to medium-rare joint. (The ends will be more well done.) **4.** Remove from the oven. Drain off the fat (dripping) from the roasting tray and reserve it. Cover the beef with foil and leave in a warm place to rest for 15 minutes. **5.** Lift the joint on to a warm serving dish and set aside while you make the gravy. **6.** Sprinkle the flour into the roasting tray and place on the heat. Stir the flour into the roasting juices, scraping the bottom well to remove any residue. Add the red wine and bubble for a few minutes, then add the stock and whisk in well. Strain into a saucepan. Bring to the boil, then simmer for a few minutes. Check the seasoning. **7.** Carve the beef and serve with the gravy, plus roast potatoes, Yorkshire puddings, some vegetables and horseradish sauce.

NOTE: Use the beef dripping for the Yorkshire puddings, which can be baked while the beef is resting.

## ROAST LOIN OF PORK
*Serves 6–8*

A middle of pork joint makes a great roast because it combines a lean cut with a fat cut. During roasting the fat from the belly bastes the loin, making it fabulously succulent, and you get really good crackling from the skin on the belly.

**I MIDDLE OF PORK JOINT (BONED
   LOIN AND BELLY), WEIGHING
   ABOUT 2KG
15 FRESH SAGE LEAVES, CHOPPED
GRATED ZEST AND JUICE OF
   I LEMON
2 GARLIC CLOVES, CHOPPED
OLIVE OIL
SALT AND BLACK PEPPER**

GRAVY
**I TBSP PLAIN WHITE FLOUR
¹/₂ GLASS WHITE WINE OR CIDER
500ML MEAT STOCK (P202)**

TO SERVE
**ROAST POTATOES (P130)
APPLE SAUCE (P136)**

**1.** With a sharp knife, score the skin of the pork at 2cm intervals. Turn the pork skin-side down. Rub the sage, lemon zest and juice, and garlic into the meat and season well with salt and black pepper. **2.** Roll the belly around the loin and tie with string at intervals to make a neat log shape. Place in a roasting tray. **3.** Dry the skin with kitchen paper, then leave uncovered in the kitchen to dry for 1 hour. **4.** Preheat the oven to 175°C. Just before you put the pork into the oven, rub the skin with oil and sprinkle with salt. **5.** Roast for 1½ hours, then turn the oven up to 200°C. Continue roasting for 30 minutes to 1 hour until the crackling is a rich golden brown and looks blistered (keep watch and turn the joint around to prevent any burning). **6.** Remove from the oven and pour off excess fat from the tray (reserve this for later use). Cover the pork with foil and leave to rest for 15 minutes. **7.** Place the pork in a warm serving dish and set aside while you make the gravy. **8.** Sprinkle the flour into the roasting tray and place on the heat. Stir the flour into the roasting juices, scraping the bottom well to remove any residue. Add the wine and bubble for a few minutes, then add the stock and whisk in well. Strain into a saucepan. Bring to the boil, then simmer for a few minutes. Check the seasoning. **9.** Cut the pork into thick slices and serve with the gravy, plus roast potatoes, some vegetables and apple sauce.

NOTE: You can use the reserved fat to cook Bubble and squeak (p45).

## ROAST CHICKEN
*Serves 4*

Higher-quality chickens – free-range and preferably organic – are worth every penny. Their meat is darker and slightly tougher than that of standard supermarket chickens, with much more flavour. Even if it means you have roast chicken less often, pay more for your bird.

I CHICKEN, WEIGHING ABOUT 2KG
I LEMON, CUT IN HALF
I GARLIC BULB, CUT IN HALF HORIZONTALLY
HANDFUL OF FRESH TARRAGON SPRIGS
2 TSP OLIVE OIL
30G BUTTER, MELTED
I TBSP PLAIN WHITE FLOUR
300ML CHICKEN STOCK (P202)
SALT AND BLACK PEPPER
POTATO GRATIN TO SERVE (P131)

1. Preheat the oven to 200°C. Season inside the chicken with salt and black pepper. Squeeze the juice from the lemon into the cavity, then put in the lemon halves together with the halved garlic and tarragon. 2. Place the bird breast up in a roasting tray. Brush with the olive oil mixed with the melted butter. Season the outside with salt and pepper. 3. Roast for 30 minutes, then reduce the heat to 150°C. Roast for a further 30–40 minutes until the chicken is cooked through. To check, cut in between a leg and the body: the juices should run clear. If they are bloody, roast for 10 more minutes. Remove the chicken from the oven and leave to rest for 15 minutes. 4. Tip out any juices from the cavity of the bird into the roasting tray. Place the bird on a carving board and keep warm. 5. Set the roasting tray on the heat. Sprinkle in the flour and stir this around to mix in any crisp bits from the tray. Add the chicken stock. Pour into a small saucepan and bring to the boil, whisking. Simmer for 5 minutes. Check the seasoning. 6. Cut the legs from the chicken and divide each one into drumstick and thigh. Remove the backbone from the bird, which will leave you with two breasts on the bone (this is called the crown). Using a heavy knife, cut the crown in half down the centre. Cut each of the breasts across into two pieces. 7. Serve the chicken with the gravy and potato gratin.

NOTE: The meat on a higher-quality chicken will be darker than that of a standard supermarket chicken, and the juices after cooking will also be darker.

## ROAST LEG OF LAMB
*Serves 6–8*

Our roast leg of lamb at Canteen is really good. Obviously the quality of the meat is paramount, and for a proper roast it's worth spending a bit. The lamb is roasted with a lot of garlic and the slow-cooked cloves become quite sweet, making a gravy that is deliciously garlicky but not too pungent.

**I BONED AND ROLLED LEG OF
   LAMB, WEIGHING ABOUT 2KG
HANDFUL OF FRESH ROSEMARY
3 GARLIC BULBS, CUT IN HALF
   HORIZONTALLY
I 1/2 TBSP OLIVE OIL
SALT AND BLACK PEPPER**

GRAVY
**I TBSP PLAIN WHITE FLOUR
300ML MEAT STOCK (P202)**

TO SERVE
**ROAST POTATOES (PI30)
MINT SAUCE (PI38)**

1. Preheat the oven to 200°C. Tuck some of the rosemary sprigs under the string all over the lamb. Season well with salt and pepper. 2. Place the garlic halves and remaining rosemary over the bottom of a roasting tray. Set the lamb on top and drizzle over the olive oil. 3. Roast for 1–1¼ hours for nice pink meat. Remove from the oven and leave to rest for 15 minutes. 4. Lift the lamb from the tray and place on a warmed serving plate. Set aside while you make the gravy. 5. Squeeze the garlic out of the papery husks. Discard any cloves that are blackened. Sprinkle the flour into the roasting tray and mix with the roasting juices and garlic, squashing it well. Whisk in the stock. Bring to the boil, then simmer for a few minutes. Strain the gravy. Check the seasoning. 6. Cut the lamb into slices and serve with the gravy plus roast potatoes, some vegetables and mint sauce.

NOTE: Ask the butcher to bone and roll the leg of lamb – it is a lot easier to carve than a leg on the bone.

## CHARGRILLED PORK CHOPS
*Serves 4*

Go to a good butcher to buy organic or free-range pork chops with a thick covering of fat, and have him cut them on the bone 3–4cm thick. If they are too thin, they will overcook and the result will be dry. Chargrilled like this you will have juicy meat with a tasty caramelised outside.

**4 LARGE PORK LOIN CHOPS, CUT
3–4CM THICK, WEIGHING
ABOUT 250G EACH
12 FRESH SAGE LEAVES
2 TSP OLIVE OIL
SALT AND BLACK PEPPER
1 LEMON, CUT INTO WEDGES**

1. Heat a cast-iron ribbed griddle pan until it is very hot. **2.** Season the chops on both sides with salt, black pepper and sage leaves. Brush with olive oil. **3.** Chargrill the chops for 5–6 minutes on one side until well browned. Turn the chops on to their skin/fat side, resting them against each other to keep them upright, and cook for 5 minutes. Lay them flat again on their other uncooked side and cook for a further 5 minutes. **4.** Place on a warmed serving dish and leave to rest for 5 minutes. **5.** Serve with any juices from the pan and a wedge of lemon to squeeze over.

NOTE: Great with Mustard butter (p136).

## CHARGRILLED LAMB CHOPS
*Serves 4*

For a simple treatment like this, your lamb chops need to be top quality. Salt marsh lamb, from the Romney Marsh and Wales, has a wonderful distinct flavour. Or you could try chops from a hogget, which is a 12-month-old lamb (halfway between lamb and mutton). These are really tasty.

**8–12 BEST END (RIB) OR LOIN LAMB
CHOPS, CUT ABOUT 3CM THICK
SPRIGS OF FRESH ROSEMARY
OLIVE OIL
SALT AND BLACK PEPPER**

1. Heat a cast-iron ribbed griddle pan until it is very hot. **2.** Season the lamb chops with a few rosemary leaves, salt and pepper. Brush lightly with oil. **3.** Chargrill for 3–4 minutes on each side for a pink chop. **4.** Leave to rest in a warm place for a few minutes before serving.

NOTE: Smoked paprika butter (p138) is a good partner for lamb chops, as is the more traditional Mint sauce (see p138).

## CHARGRILLED STEAK

Always buy the best-quality steak you can afford. Look for steak from grass-fed British-reared beef that has been hung for at least 28 days. Its flavour and texture will blow you away!

**YOUR CHOICE OF STEAK, RUMP, RIB-EYE OR SIRLOIN, CUT 2.5–3CM THICK**
**OLIVE OIL**
**SALT AND BLACK PEPPER**

**1.** Remove the steak from the fridge an hour before you want to cook it, to allow it to come to room temperature. **2.** Heat a cast-iron ribbed griddle pan until it is very hot. Or, prepare a charcoal fire – burn the charcoal until the flames have died down and the coals look greyish/white in colour. **3.** Just before cooking, season the steak well with salt and black pepper on both sides and brush lightly with oil (do not oil the pan). **4.** Chargrill the steak: 3–4 minutes in total for rare; 5–6 minutes in total for medium; 8–10 minutes in total for well done. Don't turn the steak over too many times – ideally just once – and cook for the same amount of time on each side. **5.** Leave to rest for 5 minutes before serving.

RUMP

The best flavour of all the steaks, but slightly more chewy than a sirloin. Rump is best cooked rare to medium-rare because it will become very tough if cooked any further than medium. Choose steaks 2.5–3cm thick that have been cut across the grain.

RIB-EYE

Very good flavour with quite a bit of fat running through it. Have the steak cut 2.5cm thick.

SIRLOIN

Excellent full-flavoured steak, ideally cut 3–4cm thick, with a good thick layer of fat.

## YORKSHIRE PUDDINGS

*Makes 12 to serve 6*

**100G PLAIN WHITE FLOUR**
**1/2 TSP SALT**
**3 MEDIUM EGGS**
**400–500ML MILK**
**BEEF DRIPPING (FROM THE ROAST**
    **BEEF YOU WILL BE EATING WITH**
    **THE PUDDINGS)**

**1.** Put the flour in a bowl with the salt.
Crack in the eggs and beat them in, then
slowly add the milk, beating until smooth.
The batter should have the consistency of
single cream, so add as much of the milk as
needed to achieve this. Keep in the fridge
until ready to cook. **2.** Preheat the oven
to 215°C. Put a spoonful of beef dripping
in each of 12 medium Yorkshire pudding
tins. Place in the oven to heat for about
5 minutes or until the fat is smoking.
**3.** Ladle or pour the batter into the tins,
to fill them three-quarters full. Bake for
15–18 minutes until puffed and golden
brown. Serve hot.

NOTE: If you don't have any beef dripping
you can use duck fat or even vegetable oil.

## ROAST POTATOES

*Serves 4–6*

**1.5KG FLOURY POTATOES**
    **(SEE BELOW)**
**250G DUCK OR GOOSE FAT**
**1 GARLIC BULB**
**2 SPRIGS OF FRESH ROSEMARY**
**SALT**

**1.** Preheat the oven to 200°C. Peel the
potatoes and cut each into three or four
pieces. Rinse in cold water. **2.** Put them
into a saucepan, cover with water and add
1 teaspoon salt. Bring to the boil, then
simmer for about 10 minutes or until the
potatoes are almost cooked. **3.** Drain in a
colander. Leave to cool for 5 minutes, then
toss the potatoes gently in the colander to
roughen the outsides (this will give you
perfect crisp potatoes). Place the potatoes
in a heavy roasting tin. **4.** Melt the duck
or goose fat and pour over the potatoes.
Cut the garlic bulb horizontally in half and
remove any excess papery skin (you don't
need to completely peel the halves). Add
the garlic and rosemary to the potatoes.
With your hands, gently turn them to coat
all over with the fat. Spread out in a single
layer. **5.** Roast for 40–50 minutes until
tender and browned. Turn them over twice
during this time. **6.** Drain the potatoes and
season with salt. Serve hot.

NOTES: Maris Piper potatoes are our choice
for roasting because they have a good
floury texture • Strain and reserve the duck
or goose fat. You can use it for roasting
potatoes another time, or to fry any
leftover roast potatoes with cabbage for a
perfect Bubble and squeak (p45).

## POTATO GRATIN

*Serves 4*

**1KG WAXY POTATOES, SUCH AS
    DESIREE
1 TSP SALT
500ML DOUBLE CREAM
4 GARLIC CLOVES, CHOPPED**

**1.** Preheat the oven to 175°C. Peel the potatoes and cut into thin slices (about 5mm). Do not rinse them – you need the starch in this dish. Mix the potatoes with the salt, cream and garlic. **2.** Arrange the potato slices, slightly overlapping each other, in layers in an ovenproof dish. Pour over the remainder of the cream mixture. Cover with a piece of baking parchment. **3.** Bake for 1–1¼ hours until the potatoes are tender. To test, stick a small knife into the gratin; there should be no resistance. **4.** Remove the parchment and bake uncovered for a further 15 minutes, so that the top can brown. Serve hot.

## CARROT AND SWEDE

*Serves 6*

**500G SWEDE
500G CARROTS
50G BUTTER
A FEW PINCHES OF GROUND MACE
SALT AND BLACK PEPPER**

**1.** Peel the swede and cut into 3-cm chunks. **2.** Peel the carrots and cut in half lengthways, then cut into pieces approximately half the size of the swede chunks, to ensure they cook evenly. **3.** Place the vegetables in a pan, cover with cold water and add some salt. Bring to the boil, then simmer for 20–30 minutes until tender. **4.** Drain well and tip back into the pan. Lightly crush the vegetables with a potato masher. Mix in the butter and season with plenty of pepper and the mace. Serve hot.

NOTES: You need to peel swede with a sharp knife as it has a very thick skin that is quite woody • Go easy on the mace as too much can be overpowering.

## BRAISED RED CABBAGE
*Serves 6*

I RED CABBAGE, WEIGHING
  ABOUT IKG
I EATING APPLE
2 TBSP OLIVE OIL
4 GARLIC CLOVES, CHOPPED
I TSP GROUND ALLSPICE
I TSP GROUND GINGER
1/2 TSP CAYENNE PEPPER
PINCH OF GROUND CLOVES
2 HEAPED TBSP RAISINS
2 HEAPED TBSP MUSCOVADO
  SUGAR
GRATED ZEST AND JUICE OF
  I ORANGE
80ML RED WINE VINEGAR
SALT

1. Remove the outer discoloured leaves from the cabbage. Cut it into quarters and remove the core, then shred the cabbage. **2.** Peel the apple and remove the core, then cut into dice. **3.** Heat up the olive oil in a heavy-bottomed pan that is big enough to hold all of the cabbage. Add the garlic and sauté for a few minutes until lightly browned. Be careful not to let it burn. **4.** Add the cabbage together with all the spices and cook for 5 minutes, stirring constantly. **5.** Add the apple, raisins, sugar, orange zest and juice, and salt to taste. Stir well, then mix in the vinegar and 75ml water. **6.** Cover with a lid and cook for 40 minutes, stirring from time to time. During the cooking if the mixture looks too dry, add a little more water. Serve hot.

## ROASTED FIELD MUSHROOMS
*Serves 6*

6 LARGE, FLAT FIELD
  MUSHROOMS
2 TSP OLIVE OIL
2 GARLIC CLOVES, CHOPPED
30G BUTTER
A FEW DASHES OF
  WORCESTERSHIRE SAUCE
6 SPRIGS OF FRESH THYME
SALT AND BLACK PEPPER

1. Preheat the oven to 175°C. Wipe the mushrooms with a damp cloth to clean. **2.** Rub the olive oil over the bottom of an ovenproof dish. Arrange the mushrooms, stalks up, in the dish. **3.** Scatter over the chopped garlic. Divide the butter among the mushrooms. Season with salt, pepper and Worcestershire sauce. Place a thyme sprig in each mushroom. **4.** Roast for 15 minutes.

## CABBAGE WITH BACON, LEMON AND PEPPER

*Serves 6*

**1 SAVOY CABBAGE, WEIGHING
ABOUT 1KG
150G DRY-CURE STREAKY BACON
30G BUTTER
GRATED ZEST AND JUICE OF
1 LEMON
BLACK PEPPER**

1. Remove the dark outer leaves from the cabbage and discard any that are discoloured. Cut out the cores from the dark leaves, then shred. Cut the remaining cabbage into quarters, remove the core and shred. 2. Cut the bacon into thin strips. 3. Melt the butter in a heavy-bottomed pan and fry the bacon on a medium heat for about 5 minutes or until crisp. Remove with a slotted spoon and reserve. 4. Put the cabbage into the pan and add the lemon zest and juice and a splash of water. Cover with a lid and cook for 4–5 minutes until the cabbage is just tender. 5. Remove the lid and mix the bacon bits and pepper to taste into the cabbage. Serve hot.

## MUSTARD BUTTER

*Serves 4–6*

**150G SOFT BUTTER
2 TSP ENGLISH MUSTARD POWDER
1 HEAPED TBSP GRAIN MUSTARD
1 TSP MUSTARD SEEDS**

1. Mix all the ingredients together thoroughly. Cover and chill to firm up the butter. 2. To serve, scoop out portions of butter with a spoon.

## APPLE SAUCE

*Serves 6–8*

**500G BRAMLEY APPLES
30G SUGAR, OR TO TASTE
20G BUTTER**

1. Peel the apples, cut into quarters and remove the cores. Slice the apples and place in a saucepan. 2. Sprinkle on the sugar and add the butter. Cover and cook over a low heat for 10–15 minutes until the apples fall apart, stirring occasionally. 3. This is quite a tart sauce. Taste and add more sugar if you like it a little sweeter. Serve warm.

NOTE: This can be kept in the fridge for up to 3 days.

## HORSERADISH SAUCE

*Serves at least 6*

**100G STICK OF FRESH
HORSERADISH
1/2 TSP SALT
JUICE OF 1/2 LEMON
300G CRÈME FRAÎCHE**

1. Peel the horseradish using a potato peeler. Grate it on a fine grater (such as for grating Parmesan or orange zest).
2. Season the horseradish with the salt and lemon juice and mix well, then add the crème fraîche.

NOTE: The sauce can be kept in the fridge for up to 3 days. Use leftover sauce in roast beef sandwiches.

## BREAD SAUCE

*Serves 4*

**80G STALE WHITE BREAD
300ML FULL-FAT MILK
1 SMALL ONION, SLICED
3 BAY LEAVES
3 WHOLE CLOVES
6 BLACK PEPPERCORNS
50ML DOUBLE CREAM
FRESHLY GRATED NUTMEG
PINCH OF SALT**

1. Remove the crusts from the bread, then put it in a food processor and chop into coarse crumbs. 2. Put the milk in a saucepan and add the onion, bay leaves, cloves and black peppercorns. Bring to the boil. 3. Remove from the heat, cover and leave to infuse for 30 minutes. 4. Strain the milk into a clean pan and discard the flavourings. Bring the milk back up to the boil. 5. Stir in the breadcrumbs, double cream, nutmeg to taste and salt. Serve hot.

## MINT SAUCE
*Serves at least 6–8*

**1 BUNCH OF FRESH MINT
    (ABOUT 75G)
40G CASTER SUGAR
100ML MALT VINEGAR**

**1.** Pick the leaves from the mint and chop.
**2.** Whisk the sugar with the vinegar and
100ml water to dissolve. Stir in the mint.
Serve soon after making.

## BÉARNAISE SAUCE
*Serves 4–6*

**25G FRESH TARRAGON SPRIGS
60G SHALLOTS, FINELY DICED
40ML WHITE WINE VINEGAR
1 RECIPE HOLLANDAISE SAUCE
    (P203)**

**1.** Pick the tarragon leaves and chop;
reserve the stalks. **2.** Place the shallots
in a small saucepan with the tarragon
stalks, vinegar and 40ml water. Simmer
until all liquid has evaporated and the
shallots are soft. Discard the tarragon
stalks. **3.** Mix the hollandaise sauce with
the chopped tarragon leaves and shallots.

## SMOKED PAPRIKA BUTTER
*Serves 4–6*

**150G SOFT BUTTER
2 GARLIC CLOVES, CHOPPED
GRATED ZEST OF 1/2 LEMON
1 TSP SMOKED PAPRIKA (EITHER
    SMOKED OR HOT)
2 TSP DIJON MUSTARD
A FEW SPLASHES OF TABASCO AND
    WORCESTERSHIRE SAUCES
2 TSP HORSERADISH SAUCE (P137)
10G FRESH CHIVES, FINELY
    SNIPPED**

**1.** In a bowl, mix the soft butter with all
the other ingredients until well combined.
Cover and chill to firm up the butter.
**2.** To serve, scoop out portions of butter
with a spoon.

# FISH

## FISH CAKES WITH MUSHY PEAS
*Serves 6*

The Canteen fish cake is pretty luxurious, with a high ratio of fish to potato. We serve it with mushy peas. This is not the minted green pea purée you often get. These are real mushy peas, made with dried marrowfat peas and seasoned with malt vinegar.

MUSHY PEAS

**250G DRIED MARROWFAT PEAS**
**BIG PINCH OF BICARBONATE**
  **OF SODA**
**MALT VINEGAR TO TASTE**
  **(OPTIONAL)**
**SALT AND WHITE PEPPER**

FISH CAKES

**20G BUTTER**
**1/2 ONION, FINELY DICED**
**50G FINELY DICED LEEK**
**200G SMOKED HADDOCK FILLET**
**200G WHITE FISH FILLET**
**125G LEFTOVER MASH (P87)**
**GRATED ZEST AND JUICE OF**
  **1/2 LEMON**
**20G FRESH PARSLEY, CHOPPED**
**20G FRESH CHIVES, CHOPPED**
**10G FRESH TARRAGON SPRIGS**
**15G CAPERS, CHOPPED**
**A FEW SPLASHES OF TABASCO**
  **SAUCE**
**50G SOFT BREADCRUMBS**
**SALT AND BLACK PEPPER**
**LEMON WEDGES TO SERVE**

COATING AND FRYING

**100G PLAIN WHITE FLOUR**
**2 EGGS, BEATEN WITH 3 TBSP MILK**
**250G DRIED BREADCRUMBS**
**OIL FOR SHALLOW FRYING**

**1.** Place the dried peas in a pan and cover with twice their volume of cold water. Add the bicarbonate of soda and leave to soak overnight. **2.** The next day, place the pan on the heat and bring to the boil. Simmer for about 45 minutes or until the peas are soft, stirring regularly. During cooking add more water if the pan looks too dry. **3.** Season to taste with salt and pepper plus a few splashes of malt vinegar, if you like. **4.** To make the fish cakes, melt the butter in a small saucepan and sweat the onion and leek for about 10 minutes or until soft but not brown. Allow to cool. **5.** Place the fish fillets in a deep dish and cover with boiling water. Cover the dish with cling film and leave for 10 minutes to part-cook them. Drain. Break into big pieces, discarding skin and any bones. **6.** Mix together the softened vegetables, mash, lemon zest and juice, herbs, capers, Tabasco and seasoning to taste. Gently mix in the fish and then the breadcrumbs. **7.** Divide into six and shape into cakes. For a very neat shape, press each cake into an 8cm pastry cutter. Chill for 1 hour. **8.** Gently dredge the cakes in flour, then dip in egg and, finally, roll in dried breadrumbs to coat all over. **9.** Shallow fry in 2cm of oil on a medium heat for 4 minutes on each side, then drain on kitchen paper. Meanwhile, reheat the mushy peas. **10.** Serve the fish cakes with lemon wedges and the mushy peas.

NOTES: Part-cooking, rather than completely cooking, the fish, and then mixing it at the end, will ensure that you have nice chunks of fish in your fish cakes • You can use any meaty white fish fillet, such as coley, pollock, whiting and ling.

## GRILLED GURNARD WITH BACON AND SPRING ONION MASH

*Serves 4*

This dish has it all covered from a taste point of view. Gurnard may look like a Mediterranean fish, but it's caught in British waters. It is meaty with a good strong flavour, and has always been a favourite at Canteen.

**4 GURNARD FILLETS, WEIGHING
200–250G EACH
1 1/2 TBSP OLIVE OIL
30G BUTTER, MELTED
SALT AND BLACK PEPPER
LEMON WEDGES TO SERVE**

MASH
**800G FLOURY POTATOES, SUCH
AS MARIS PIPER
100G BUTTER, MELTED
200G DRY-CURE STREAKY BACON
1 BUNCH OF SPRING ONIONS,
SHREDDED**

1. To make the mash, peel the potatoes and cut into 1cm slices. Rinse under cold running water for 5 minutes. Place in a pan, cover with cold water and add some salt. Bring to the boil, then cook for about 15 minutes or until tender. 2. Preheat the oven to 200°C. Preheat the grill. 3. Drain the potatoes, reserving the cooking water. Put the potatoes through a mouli (vegetable mill) or potato ricer into a clean pan. Beat in the melted butter and add a little of the cooking water if the mash seems too thick. 4. Grill the bacon until crisp, then cut into thin strips. Beat the bacon and spring onions into the mash and season with plenty of black pepper. Cover and keep warm. (Reheat for serving, if necessary.) 5. Remove any pin bones from the fish fillets with tweezers. Season the fish with salt and black pepper. Pour the oil on to a baking sheet that is big enough to hold the fish side by side. Pour over the melted butter. Turn the fish over in the butter and oil to coat evenly, then turn skin-side up. 6. Place under the hot grill and cook for 4–5 minutes until the skin is starting to scorch a little. Transfer to the oven to finish cooking for 3–4 minutes. 7. Serve the fish with the mash and a wedge of lemon. Spoon some of the fish cooking liquid over too.

NOTE: You can leave the bacon out of the mash if you don't eat meat.

## FISH AND CHIPS WITH TARTARE SAUCE
*Serves 4*

We all have happy memories of eating fish and chips from a paper wrapping, sitting on the seafront, but it's fair to say that today it's hard to find good fish and chips. Ours ARE good. The fish is breaded, so is light, crisp and less greasy than battered fish, and the generously cut chips are crunchy on the outside, tender within.

**4 SKINLESS WHITE FISH FILLETS (YOU CAN USE POLLOCK, COD, WHITING OR PLAICE), WEIGHING ABOUT 200G EACH**
**PLAIN WHITE FLOUR**
**2 EGGS, BEATEN AND SEASONED WITH SALT**
**200G FINE, DRIED WHITE BREADCRUMBS (OR MATZOMEAL)**
**SEA SALT**

CHIPS
**IKG MARIS PIPER POTATOES**
**VEGETABLE OIL FOR DEEP-FRYING**

TO SERVE
**TARTARE SAUCE (P206)**
**LEMON WEDGES**

1. Start with the chips. Peel the potatoes and cut into chips of equal thickness – about 1cm. Quickly rinse in cold water and drain, then dry with kitchen paper or a tea towel. 2. Pour oil into a large, heavy-bottomed pan (or a deep-fryer) to fill it no more than one-third full. Heat up the oil to 140°C. 3. Fry the chips in a basket in three batches for 4–6 minutes until they are just soft inside. They should not be at all crisp at this stage. 4. Tip them onto a tray in a thin layer so that they will cool down more quickly. Keep aside until you are ready for the next stage (this part can be done in advance). 5. Toss the fish in flour, then dip into egg, ensuring it is coated all over, and finally coat evenly with breadcrumbs. Place on a tray, in one layer and not touching, and keep in the fridge until needed. 6. When you are ready to cook, preheat the oven to 175°C. 7. Heat the pan of oil to 180°C. Add the fish and deep-fry for 4–5 minutes until golden brown and crisp on both sides. Drain on kitchen paper and sprinkle with sea salt. Keep hot in the oven while you finish the chips. 8. Heat up the oil to 190°C. Deep-fry the chips in batches for 2–3 minutes until crisp and golden. Drain on kitchen paper and sprinkle with salt. 9. Serve the fish and chips with tartare sauce and lemon wedges.

NOTES: If your fish fillets are thick, reduce the temperature of the oil to 170°C and deep-fry for 6–7 minutes • When frying the chips, bring the oil back up to the required temperature between batches.

## SKATE WITH BLACK BUTTER
*Serves 4*

Anybody who avoids eating fish should try skate because there are no sharp bones to worry about and the flesh is firm and meaty. It's an easy fish to cook, not at all intimidating. Really delicious as prepared here.

**4 PORTIONS OF SKATE WING,**
**    4–5CM AT THICKEST POINT,**
**    WEIGHING 250–300G EACH**
**1 1/2 TBSP OLIVE OIL**
**100G BUTTER**
**30G CAPERS**
**1 LEMON, HALVED**
**25G FRESH PARSLEY, CHOPPED**
**SALT AND BLACK PEPPER**
**LEMON WEDGES TO SERVE**

**1.** With a heavy knife, cut out the bone at the thick end of the skate wings. Trim off 1cm of the wing tips using kitchen scissors. (You could ask your fishmonger to do all this preparation for you.) Season the fish on both sides with salt and pepper.
**2.** Heat up a very large frying pan with the olive oil. Add half the butter and sizzle until it has all melted. Place the skate in the pan and cook for 4 minutes on each side. If it browns too quickly turn down the heat slightly. **3.** To test if the fish is done, press it with your finger at the thickest point – the flesh should come away from the bone slightly. Place on a warm serving dish.
**4.** Put the rest of the butter in the pan and melt it, then cook until it is a light brown colour. **5.** Throw in the capers and cook for 1 minute. Squeeze in the juice from the lemon halves and add the parsley.
**6.** Pour the butter mixture over the skate and serve with the lemon wedges.

## WHOLE GRILLED BLACK BREAM OR SEABASS

*Serves 4*

We are all keen sea fishermen, and know that there is nothing better than eating a spanking fresh fish you have caught yourself. This is how we like to prepare our fish – in the simplest way. Black bream is a strong-flavoured fish so it really doesn't need a sauce.

**4 WHOLE WILD BLACK BREAM OR SEABASS, WEIGHING 350–500G EACH (SEE NOTE)**
**75ML OLIVE OIL**
**SALT AND BLACK PEPPER**
**2 LEMONS, HALVED**

**1.** Preheat the oven to 200°C. Preheat the grill. Cut three or four 1-cm-deep slashes on each side of the fish, but not going all the way to the bone. Season well inside and out. **2.** Place the fish on a baking sheet and drizzle with olive oil. Turn the fish over a few times to make sure it is covered in oil. **3.** Grill for 4–5 minutes until browning. Transfer to the oven to finish cooking for 10–12 minutes. To check if the fish is done, press along the backbone – the flesh will come away from the bone when it is ready. **4.** Serve hot with lemon halves.

NOTE: You can ask your fishmonger to prepare the fish for you, but if you want to clean and scale it yourself, here's how. First, with a sharp knife cut a slit from the anal fin all the way to the gills, cutting along the belly. Pull out all the guts. To remove the scales you can use a special descaler or a small, blunt serrated knife. It is quite a messy job, and a good way to do it is under water! Place a large chopping board in the sink, resting one end on the edge of the sink. Fill the sink with water. Set the fish, head down, on its one side on the board – you want it to be immersed in water – and scrape away from you. Turn it on to its other side and scrape off the scales there. Doing it this way should stop the scales from flying all over the kitchen. Finally, with a pair of scissors cut off all fins and spines, and rinse the fish well inside and out.

## SMOKED HADDOCK, SPINACH AND MASH
*Serves 4*

You could say this is like a deconstructed fish pie, with all the elements served side by side rather than being piled up. It's quite a simple dish to prepare. We prefer to use undyed smoked haddock with its subtle natural colour and flavour from the smoking.

**800G FLOURY POTATOES, SUCH AS MARIS PIPER**
**150G BUTTER, MELTED**
**4 UNDYED SMOKED HADDOCK FILLETS, WEIGHING ABOUT 200G EACH**
**BUTTER FOR COOKING THE FISH**
**SALT AND BLACK PEPPER**

SPINACH
**500G SPINACH**
**OLIVE OIL**
**FRESHLY GRATED NUTMEG**
**20G BUTTER**

TO SERVE
**LEMON WEDGES**
**HOLLANDAISE SAUCE (P203)**

1. Peel the potatoes and cut into 1-cm thick slices. Rinse in cold water. Place in a pan, cover with water and add some salt. Bring to the boil, then cook for about 15 minutes or until tender. 2. Preheat the grill. 3. Drain the potatoes well, reserving some of the cooking liquid. Return the potatoes to the pan and mash with a hand masher. Whisk in the melted butter and a little of the cooking water to make the mash consistency you like. Cover and keep warm. 4. Butter a baking sheet and place the haddock fillets on it. Dot with a little more butter and season with black pepper. Cook under the grill for 5–6 minutes until done. To test, press gently with a fork – the flesh should slightly separate into flakes. 5. While the fish is cooking, heat up a pan large enough to hold the spinach. When it is very hot add a splash of olive oil and throw in the spinach. Turn it over with tongs for 1–2 minutes until wilted. 6. Tip into a colander and press out any excess liquid. Return to the pan and season with a few gratings of nutmeg, pepper to taste and the butter. 7. Serve the haddock with the mash, spinach and lemon wedges, with hollandaise sauce on the side.

NOTE: This is also good with Parsley sauce (p205) in place of hollandaise, or you can serve it without any sauce.

## SOUSED MACKEREL

*Serves 6*

There are loads of mackerel in English waters in the summer, and they're easy to catch. Sousing – soaking in a spiced pickling liquid – is a good way to prepare them. The souse here is slightly sweet/sour, which is a good foil for the rich fish.

**6 MACKEREL FILLETS**
**2 TSP SALT**
**BOILED NEW POTATOES TO SERVE**

SOUSE

**1 LEMON**
**1 ORANGE**
**100G SHALLOTS, THINLY SLICED**
**70G CARROT, HALVED**
    **LENGTHWAYS AND THINLY**
    **SLICED**
**70G FENNEL, THINLY SLICED**
**4 GARLIC CLOVES, THINLY SLICED**
**40G CASTER SUGAR**
**10 WHITE PEPPERCORNS**
**20 CORIANDER SEEDS**
**1 DRIED RED CHILLI**
**1 STAR ANISE**
**6 BAY LEAVES**
**150ML CIDER VINEGAR**

**1.** Lay the mackerel fillets in a large flat dish and sprinkle salt over both sides. Spread out the fillets in a single layer, cover and leave for 3–4 hours. **2.** With a peeler, cut thin strips of peel from the lemon and orange, then squeeze out the juice. **3.** Put all the souse ingredients, with the lemon and orange peel and juice, in a stainless-steel pan. Add 100ml water and bring to the boil. Simmer for 3 minutes, then remove from the heat. Allow to cool. **4.** Drain off any liquid from the fish. Pour over the cool souse. Shake the dish to get the liquid everywhere, then cover and refrigerate for 12 hours. **5.** Serve the fish with some of the souse vegetables and boiled new potatoes.

NOTE: Other oily fish, such as herring, can be soused in the same way.

## HERRING AND POTATO SALAD
*Serves 4*

This is a fabulous warm salad: rich oily herring, potatoes that have soaked up the strong mustardy flavours of the dressing, gherkins and capers to add a sweet-sharp edge, and a touch of sour cream to finish.

**500G NEW POTATOES, SUCH AS
    JERSEY ROYALS, ROSEVAL OR
    DESIREE, SCRUBBED
40G GHERKINS
20G CAPERS
5 TBSP MUSTARD DRESSING (P206)
4 FRESH HERRINGS, FILLETED
OLIVE OIL
20G FRESH CHIVES, SNIPPED
80G SOUR CREAM
SALT AND BLACK PEPPER
LEMON WEDGES TO SERVE**

1. Put the potatoes in a pan, cover with cold water and add some salt. Bring to the boil, then simmer gently until just tender.
2. Preheat the grill. Drain the potatoes and cut into quarters. Put into a bowl. 3. Chop the gherkins and capers and toss with the potatoes and mustard dressing. Set aside.
4. Season the fish fillets with salt and pepper and brush lightly with olive oil. Grill skin-side up for 3–4 minutes until cooked and lightly scorched. 5. Mix the chives and sour cream into the potato salad. 6. Serve the fish with the potato salad and lemon wedges.

## MUSSELS WITH CIDER AND PARSLEY
*Serves 2–3*

Just like oysters, mussels were once the food of the poor in these islands. This way of preparing them is a West Country twist on the classic French *moules marinière*, using dry cider (preferably from Somerset).

**1KG MUSSELS
20G BUTTER
50G SHALLOTS, DICED
2 GARLIC CLOVES, CHOPPED
100ML DRY CIDER
80ML DOUBLE CREAM
20G FRESH PARSLEY, CHOPPED
CRUSTY BREAD TO SERVE**

1. To prepare the mussels, remove the beards and scrape off any barnacles. Discard any mussels that stay open or that have broken shells. Wash well under cold running water. 2. Heat up the butter in a large heavy-bottomed pan and sweat the shallots and garlic for a few minutes until soft but not brown. 3. Place the mussels in the pan and pour in the cider. Cover the pan tightly and cook on a high heat for 3–4 minutes until the mussels are open, shaking the pan a few times. 4. Discard any mussels that stay stubbornly shut, then add the cream and parsley. Bring to the boil and serve, with crusty bread.

NOTE: We like Westons cider.

CHAPTER 4

# PUDDINGS AND DESSERTS

## STEAMED SYRUP PUDDING

*Serves 4–6*

No one can resist this – it really went down a treat when we were testing the recipes for the book. At Canteen we make individual puddings, but we think this big one works better as you get more syrup!

**200G SOFT BUTTER, PLUS EXTRA FOR GREASING**
**200G CASTER SUGAR**
**3 EGGS**
**GRATED ZEST OF 2 LEMONS**
**35ML LEMON JUICE**
**230G SELF-RAISING WHITE FLOUR**
**I TSP BAKING POWDER**
**PINCH OF SALT**
**250G GOLDEN SYRUP**
**CREAM OR CUSTARD (P207) TO SERVE**

1. Cream the butter with the sugar until pale and fluffy. 2. Whisk the eggs, then slowly beat into the creamed mixture until smooth. 3. Add the lemon zest and juice and mix well. Sift together the flour, baking powder and salt, then fold into the mixture until combined. 4. Butter a 1-litre pudding basin and pour in the golden syrup. Spoon in the sponge mix. 5. Fold a piece of greaseproof paper in two to double thickness and place on top of the basin. Tie on under the rim with string. 6. Cook in a steamer with a close-fitting lid for 1 hour. 7. Lift out the basin and remove the paper. Place your serving plate (upside down) on top of the basin and hold them tightly together with a cloth, then turn them over so that the plate is the right way up. Lift off the basin, to leave the pudding on the plate. 8. Serve with a big jug of cream or custard.

## APPLE BRANDY SYLLABUB
*Serves 4–6*

We are big fans of Somerset apple brandy, which is made from cider apples in the Calvados style. It makes a delectable syllabub, which is an ancient British pud dating from the 16th century. This is a good boozy pudding, not one for the kids.

**100ML DRY CIDER**
**70G PEELED AND DICED BRAMLEY
  APPLE**
**GRATED ZEST AND JUICE OF
  1 ORANGE**
**25G MUSCOVADO SUGAR**
**4 WHOLE CLOVES**
**1 MACE BLADE**
**1/2 CINNAMON STICK**
**50ML SOMERSET APPLE BRANDY**
**275ML DOUBLE CREAM**
**SHORTBREAD (P190) TO SERVE**

1. Place the cider, apple, orange zest and juice, sugar and spices in a small stainless-steel saucepan. Cover and bring to the boil, then remove from the heat and allow to cool. 2. When cool add the apple brandy. Chill. Place a stainless-steel bowl in the fridge to chill. 3. Strain the apple mixture through a fine sieve into the chilled bowl. Add the double cream. Whisk gently by hand until the mixture thickens into ribbons but can still be poured. 4. Pour the syllabub into four to six dessert glasses and tap gently to level. Cover individually with cling film. Keep in the fridge for 3–4 hours. 5. Serve with fingers of shortbread.

## RICE PUDDING WITH JAM
*Serves 6*

Luxurious, creamy, not too sweet or stodgy, this is a perfect rice pudding. It's made on the stovetop, rather than being baked, so no skin forms (like Marmite, some people love the skin while others hate it).

**150G ARBORIO RICE**
**900ML FULL-FAT MILK**
**300ML DOUBLE CREAM**
**1 1/2 VANILLA PODS, SPLIT OPEN
  LENGTHWAYS**
**60G CASTER SUGAR**
**FRESHLY GRATED NUTMEG**
**RASPBERRY JAM TO SERVE (P213)**

1. Combine the rice with the milk, cream and split vanilla pods in a heavy saucepan. Cook on a very low heat for about 1¼ hours or until the rice is soft, stirring frequently. 2. Stir in the sugar and a few gratings of nutmeg. Remove the vanilla pods. 3. Serve the rice pudding hot, topping each portion with a dollop of jam.

NOTE: Other good toppings for rice pud are golden syrup, demerara sugar, fresh berries and rhubarb compote (see p38 for a recipe).

## BLACKCURRANT JELLY
## WITH ICE CREAM
*Serves 6*

At every children's party there will be jelly and ice cream, and we have found that big children (i.e. adults) love it too. Of course, making the jelly with fresh fruit gives a fabulous, more 'sophisticated' flavour, so much better than those jelly blocks – which we all used to like to eat raw.

**5 GELATINE LEAVES**
**150G SUGAR**
**500G BLACKCURRANTS**

TO SERVE
**VANILLA ICE CREAM (P171)**
**SHORTBREAD (P190)**

1. Put the gelatine leaves in a little cold water and leave to soak until soft.
2. Meanwhile, put the sugar in a saucepan with 300ml cold water. Bring to the boil, stirring to dissolve the sugar. Add the blackcurrants and simmer for 10 minutes.
3. Sieve the blackcurrant mixture into a bowl to remove the seeds. Measure the blackcurrant liquid – you should have 600ml. (Add a little water if necessary to top up to this amount.) 4. Squeeze the excess water out of the gelatine, then add to the blackcurrant liquid and whisk in. Sieve the mixture again. 5. Divide among six dessert glasses or pour into a serving bowl. Cover and chill for at least 6 hours to set. 6. Serve with vanilla ice cream and shortbread.

NOTE: If you don't want to make ice cream, use a good-quality shop-bought vanilla such as Green & Black's or Hellsett Farm.

## GINGERBREAD WITH PEARS
*Serves 6–8*

This dessert has a perfect balance of flavours: spicy, sticky gingerbread, sweet pears and slightly sour crème fraîche. The pears are poached in the West Country pear cider called perry. Be sure to use a dry perry – many available now are very sweet.

### GINGERBREAD
**175ML DARK TREACLE**
**250G BUTTER, PLUS EXTRA FOR GREASING**
**175G MUSCOVADO SUGAR**
**50G MARMALADE (IF YOU WANT TO MAKE YOUR OWN, SEE THE RECIPE ON P213)**
**50G CRYSTALLISED GINGER OR STEM GINGER IN SYRUP, VERY FINELY CHOPPED**
**250G PLAIN WHITE FLOUR**
**2 TSP BAKING POWDER**
**4 TSP GROUND GINGER**
**2 TSP GROUND CINNAMON**
**4 MEDIUM EGGS**
**175ML MILK**
**75G CRÈME FRAÎCHE**

### POACHED PEARS
**PARED ZEST AND JUICE OF 1 LEMON**
**500ML DRY PERRY**
**70G CASTER SUGAR**
**1KG FIRM PEARS**
**1 VANILLA POD, SPLIT OPEN LENGTHWAYS**

### TO SERVE
**ICING SUGAR**
**CRÈME FRAÎCHE**

**1.** Preheat the oven to 160°C. Combine the treacle, butter, sugar, marmalade and chopped ginger in a saucepan and bring to the boil. **2.** Sift the flour, baking powder and spices into a mixing bowl. **3.** Whisk together the eggs, milk and crème fraîche in another bowl. Slowly pour in the hot treacle mix, whisking constantly. Fold in the sifted dry ingredients. **4.** Butter a large, deep metal tin that is 30 x 20cm and 6cm deep. Line with baking parchment. Pour in the gingerbread mixture. **5.** Bake for about 40 minutes or until a skewer inserted into the centre comes out clean. Allow to cool. **6.** When cold, remove from the tray. Wrap in baking parchment and then with cling film. **7.** Next prepare the pears. Put the lemon zest and juice into a bowl with the perry and sugar. Peel and quarter the pears. Remove the cores. Put them into the perry mix as you prepare them – this will prevent discoloration. **8.** Tip the pears and liquid into a saucepan and add the vanilla pod. Simmer for 15–20 minutes until the pears are just tender. Remove the pears with a slotted spoon and put to one side. Bring the poaching liquid to the boil and reduce to a syrup. Pour this over the pears and allow to cool. **9.** When ready to serve, preheat the oven to 170°C. Cut the gingerbread into squares and warm in the oven for a few minutes. **10.** Sprinkle the gingerbread with icing sugar and serve with the pears and crème fraîche.

NOTES: The gingerbread can be made well in advance and it will improve in flavour over a few days • If perry isn't available, you can use cider to poach the pears.

## PEAR AND ALMOND TART
*Makes a 25cm tart*

This is a versatile tart for all seasons
– simply change the fruits throughout
the year to whatever is best at the time.
Summer fruits like apricots, peaches or
nectarines don't need poaching first.

**25CM SWEET PASTRY CASE, BAKED
   BLIND (P208)
30G FLAKED ALMONDS**

ALMOND PASTE
**150G SOFT BUTTER
150G CASTER SUGAR
2 EGGS
4 TSP AMARETTO LIQUEUR
40G PLAIN WHITE FLOUR
150G GROUND ALMONDS
1/2 TSP SALT**

POACHED PEARS
**3 FIRM PEARS
JUICE OF 1/2 LEMON
50G CASTER SUGAR**

1. To make the almond paste, beat the
butter with the sugar until pale and fluffy.
Lightly beat the eggs with the Amaretto,
then beat into the butter and sugar mix.
Fold in the flour, ground almonds and salt.
2. Peel, quarter and core the pears. Place
in a pan with the lemon juice, sugar and
enough water to cover. Simmer for 10–15
minutes until just tender. Drain and cool.
3. Preheat the oven to 160°C. Spoon the
almond paste into the tart case, spreading
it evenly. 4. Arrange the quartered pears
on top of the almond paste, pushing them
in slightly. Scatter over the flaked almonds.
5. Bake for 30–40 minutes until golden
and slightly puffed up. Serve warm.

## VANILLA ICE CREAM
*Serves 6*

Vanilla pods are just magical. Using them
to make ice cream means you have lovely
flecks of black (the vanilla seeds) in the
white, and an incomparable deep, real
vanilla taste. This ice cream is so versatile –
good with just about every cake and dessert
as well as on its own.

**500ML FULL-FAT MILK
200ML DOUBLE CREAM
1 VANILLA POD
6 EGG YOLKS
170G CASTER SUGAR**

1. Put the milk and cream in a heavy
saucepan. Split open the vanilla pod and
scrape out the seeds into the pan. Cut the
pod into small pieces with scissors and
add to the pan. Bring just to the boil.
Remove from the heat and leave to infuse
for 1–2 hours. 2. Whisk together the
egg yolks and sugar in a bowl until thick
and foamy. 3. Bring the milk and cream
mixture back to the boil, then slowly
pour over the egg mixture, whisking to
combine. 4. Pour back into the pan and
cook on a low heat, stirring constantly with
a wooden spoon, until the custard coats the
back of the spoon. Do not let the custard
boil. Strain and allow to cool, then chill.
5. Churn in an ice-cream machine until
softly set, then place in the freezer to set
firm. Before serving, allow the ice cream to
soften slightly.

## CUSTARD TART WITH PRUNES
*Makes a 25cm tart*

Prunes and custard either make you groan or smack your lips. We love this combination, and thought that slightly spiced poached prunes would go well with a traditional custard tart. See what you think.

**25CM SWEET PASTRY CASE, BAKED BLIND (P208)**

FILLING

**450ML WHIPPING CREAM**
**45G SUGAR**
**5 EGG YOLKS**
**1 TSP FRESHLY GRATED NUTMEG**

PRUNES

**100G PRUNES**
**25G MUSCOVADO SUGAR**
**1/2 CINNAMON STICK**
**PARED ZEST AND JUICE OF 1 ORANGE**

1. To make the tart filling, combine the cream and sugar in a pan and bring to the boil. Remove from the heat and leave to cool for 30 minutes. 2. Preheat the oven to 125°C. Whisk the egg yolks in a bowl. Pour in the sweet cream and whisk to mix, then strain this custard into a jug. 3. Place the tart case, in its tin, on the pulled-out oven shelf. Fill with custard right to the top. Grate over the nutmeg. 4. Gently push the shelf back into the oven and bake for 25–35 minutes until just set. Allow to cool. 5. For the prunes, combine all the ingredients in a pan with 100ml water. Cover and bring to the boil, then simmer for 5 minutes. Remove from the heat and leave to cool, still covered. 6. To serve, remove the tart from the tin and cut into wedges. Serve each person some prunes and liquid alongside.

## TREACLE TART WITH CLOTTED CREAM

*Makes a 25cm tart*

Treacle tarts are often too sweet. Ours is not overpoweringly sugary, and has a slightly caramelised top with an almost nutty taste. It is so popular at Canteen that we are always having to make more.

**25CM SWEET PASTRY CASE, BAKED BLIND (P208)**
**CLOTTED CREAM TO SERVE**

FILLING
**120G STALE WHITE BREAD WITH CRUSTS**
**250ML DOUBLE CREAM**
**2 EGG YOLKS**
**200ML GOLDEN SYRUP**
**2 TSP SYRUP FROM A JAR OF STEM GINGER**
**40G BUTTER, MELTED**
**GRATED ZEST AND JUICE OF 1 LEMON**

1. Preheat the oven to 160°C. Place the bread in a food processor and process until it is in coarse crumbs. 2. Beat together the cream, egg yolks, golden and ginger syrups, melted butter and lemon zest and juice. Mix in the breadcrumbs. 3. Pour into the tart case. Bake for about 30 minutes or until golden. Allow to cool and set. 4. Just before serving, place the tart in a moderate oven to warm for 10–15 minutes. 5. Remove from the tin and cut into wedges. Serve with clotted cream.

NOTES: You could also serve the tart with Jersey cream, Vanilla ice cream (p171), Custard (p207) or crème fraîche • If you don't have a jar of stem ginger in syrup, use a big pinch of ground ginger instead.

## APPLE CRUMBLE WITH CUSTARD
*Serves 6*

All Brits love a crumble. And it turns out that visitors from other countries love it too – the French call it 'le crumble' and come to Canteen to eat ours. When we take it off the menu in the summer, we get a lot of grumbling.

**IKG BRAMLEY APPLES**
**175G CASTER SUGAR**
**PINCH OF GROUND CINNAMON**
**CUSTARD (P207) TO SERVE**

CRUMBLE
**375G PLAIN WHITE FLOUR**
**BIG PINCH OF SALT**
**120G CASTER SUGAR**
**190G COLD BUTTER, CUT IN CUBES**

1. To make the crumble topping, put the flour, salt and sugar in a bowl. Add the butter cubes and toss to coat. Leave for 30 minutes. 2. Rub together until the mixture is in fine crumbs, then continue rubbing until it starts to form bigger lumps. 3. Preheat the oven to 160°C. Peel the apples, cut in quarters and remove the cores. Cut into 1cm slices and toss with 150g of the sugar and the cinnamon. 4. Place the apples in an ovenproof dish and pour over the crumble mix, spreading it evenly. Sprinkle on the remaining caster sugar. 5. Bake for about 40 minutes or until golden and bubbling around the edges. Serve with a jug of custard.

NOTE: You could add some blackberries or blackcurrant to the apples.

## ETON MESS
*Serves 6*

No one can resist this posh pud of crushed meringues mixed with the classic combination of sweet British summer strawberries and whipped cream. You need to serve it as soon as possible, otherwise the meringues will melt away.

**500G STRAWBERRIES**
**350ML DOUBLE CREAM**

MERINGUE
**4 MEDIUM EGG WHITES**
**I TSP WHITE WINE VINEGAR**
**2 TSP BOILING WATER**
**200G CASTER SUGAR**

1. First make the meringue. Preheat the oven to 110°C. Whisk the egg whites with the vinegar and boiling water using an electric mixer for 1 minute. Add the sugar slowly, whisking constantly, then continue to whisk for 8–10 minutes until stiff and shiny. 2. Line a baking sheet with greaseproof paper. Spoon the meringue mix on to the sheet in blobs roughly the size of a lemon. Space them well apart to allow them room to expand. 3. Dry out in the oven for 2 hours. Allow to cool. 4. Remove the hulls from the strawberries, then rinse and pat dry with kitchen paper. Cut into slices and place in a bowl. 5. Whip the cream in a cold metal bowl to soft peaks. 6. Break the meringues into coarse chunks and mix with the strawberries. 7. Gently fold in the whipped cream and serve immediately.

NOTE: You can make the meringues well in advance. They will keep well in an airtight container.

## RHUBARB AND ALMOND TRIFLE
*Serves 6*

This much-loved English dessert was originally more like a fool. Later, as it became more like the trifle we know today, it was topped with frothy syllabub rather than whipped cream. The Canteen trifle is both modern and traditional, with booze-soaked cake, a fruit compote, custard and cream.

RHUBARB COMPOTE

**400G FORCED HOTHOUSE RHUBARB**
**75G CASTER SUGAR**
**A FEW THIN SLICES OF FRESH GINGER**
**PARED ZEST AND JUICE OF 1 ORANGE**

CUSTARD

**400ML MILK**
**100ML DOUBLE CREAM**
**1 VANILLA POD**
**2 EGG YOLKS**
**30G CASTER SUGAR**
**20G CORNFLOUR**

TO ASSEMBLE

**200G PLAIN SPONGE CAKE**
**40ML AMARETTO LIQUEUR**
**250ML DOUBLE CREAM**
**40G FLAKED ALMONDS, LIGHTLY TOASTED**

**1.** To make the compote, trim the rhubarb and cut into 2-cm chunks. Place in a stainless-steel pan and add the sugar, sliced ginger, and orange zest and juice. Toss together. Cover and cook over a low heat for about 10 minutes or until just tender but not falling apart. Allow to cool. **2.** Put the milk and cream in a heavy saucepan. Split the vanilla pod lengthways and scrape the seeds into the milk and cream. Add the pod too. Bring just to the boil, then remove from the heat and leave to infuse for 30 minutes. **3.** Whisk together the egg yolks, sugar and cornflour in a metal bowl. Pour over the milk and cream mix, whisking constantly. Pour back into the pan and gently bring back to the boil, stirring constantly. Strain through a sieve into a bowl. Cover the surface with silicone paper or baking parchment and allow to cool slightly before using. **4.** Cut the sponge into cubes. Place in a glass bowl, or divide among six small glass bowls if you want to serve individually. Splash over the Amaretto to moisten the sponge. **5.** Pour over the rhubarb compote, followed by the custard. Chill for 3–4 hours to set. **6.** Whip the cream until thick. Spoon it over the top of the trifle. Scatter the almonds over the cream.

NOTES: It's better if the sponge cake is a few days old because it will absorb all the rhubarb juices and Amaretto • If you don't want to make the rhubarb compote, try raspberries instead and replace the Amaretto with Madeira or medium sherry.

## CHRISTMAS PUDDING
*Makes two 1kg puddings*

This recipe has been handed down from Cass's grandmother to his mother and now to us – we make it at Canteen every year. It is a rich, spicy pudding, dense with fruit and containing very little flour. Hidden sixpence not guaranteed.

### DAY 1

**60G GLACÉ CHERRIES, HALVED**
**60G DRIED APRICOTS, CHOPPED**
**120G STONED PRUNES, CHOPPED**
**80G CURRANTS**
**170G SULTANAS**
**225G RAISINS**
**80G DICED CANDIED PEEL**
**60G BLANCHED ALMONDS,**
   **ROUGHLY CHOPPED**
**160G SOFT LIGHT BROWN SUGAR**
**140G GOLDEN SYRUP**
**90G GRATED CARROTS**
**150G GRATED BRAMLEY APPLE**
**GRATED ZEST AND JUICE OF**
   **1 LEMON**
**GRATED ZEST AND JUICE OF**
   **1 ORANGE**
**125ML BARLEY WINE**
**125ML STOUT**
**1/2 TSP EACH OF GROUND MACE,**
   **FRESHLY GRATED NUTMEG,**
   **GROUND CINNAMON AND**
   **GROUND ALLSPICE**

### DAY 2

**60G PLAIN WHITE FLOUR**
**60G SOFT WHITE BREADCRUMBS**
**60G GROUND ALMONDS**
**2 EGGS**
**80G SHREDDED SUET**

**1.** Mix together all the Day 1 ingredients. Cover and leave for 24 hours. **2.** Add the Day 2 ingredients. Mix everything together until well combined, then make a wish! **3.** Divide the mixture between two 1kg pudding basins. If using plastic basins, simply put on the lids. If you are using traditional basins, cover with a double layer of baking parchment tied on under the rim with string. **4.** Place the basins in a large steamer or in one or two pans. Add enough water to come halfway up the sides of the basins. Cover tightly and bring the water to a simmer. Steam for 4 hours, checking the water level regularly and topping up if necessary. **5.** Allow to cool, then store until Christmas in a cool, dry place. **6.** On Christmas Day, steam the pudding again for 2½ hours. Turn out and serve flaming with brandy, if you like, and with Custard (p207) or brandy butter.

NOTE: Give the second pudding away as a gift, or keep it for the following Christmas – store it in a cool, dry place or the fridge. You might want to spike it now and again with a little brandy.

## CHAPTER 5

# CAKES
# AND
# BISCUITS

## CHEESECAKE AND HAZELNUT BRITTLE
### *Makes a 25cm cheesecake*

A nut brittle is simply caramelised sugar and nuts allowed to set hard. The brittle here, made with whole hazelnuts, has a nice toasty flavour from the browned nuts and isn't too sweet. It gives a satisfyingly crunchy topping to this creamy baked cheesecake.

**200G HOBNOBS OR DIGESTIVE BISCUITS**
**60G BUTTER, MELTED**
**600G FULL-FAT SOFT CHEESE**
**150G CASTER SUGAR**
**2 EGGS**
**2 TSP PURE VANILLA EXTRACT**
**GRATED ZEST AND JUICE OF 1 LEMON**
**15G CORNFLOUR**
**170ML THICK CREAM**

HAZELNUT BRITTLE
**100G SUGAR**
**100G BLANCHED HAZELNUTS**

**1.** Preheat the oven to 170°C. Use baking parchment to line the bottom of a 25cm cake tin with a removable base. Line the side of the tin with a separate strip of parchment. **2.** Crush the biscuits in a plastic bag using a rolling pin. Tip into a bowl and mix in the melted butter. **3.** Press the mixture evenly over the bottom of the tin. Bake for 10 minutes. Remove from the oven. Turn the heat up to 150°C. **4.** Cream together the soft cheese and sugar until smooth. Beat in the eggs, vanilla extract, lemon zest and juice, and cornflour until just mixed. Stir in the cream. **5.** Pour the filling into the tin. Bake for 45 minutes. **6.** Allow to cool, then carefully remove the cheesecake from the tin and set it on a serving plate. Keep in the fridge. **7.** To make the brittle, put the sugar in a heavy-bottomed saucepan and add 2 tablespoons water. Heat slowly until all the sugar has melted, then add the nuts. Cook until the sugar starts to turn golden brown. **8.** As soon as it is golden brown, pour it onto an oiled baking sheet. You will need to be very quick at this stage so the brittle doesn't burn, which would make it taste bitter. Allow to cool. When cold, break into chunks with your fingers. **9.** Scatter the nut brittle over the top of the cheesecake before serving.

## CHOCOLATE BEETROOT CAKE
*Makes a 28cm cake*

People are intrigued by this cake. The beetroot flavour is very subtle and you wouldn't identify it if you didn't know what it was. It works really well with chocolate. Because the cake is made with oil, not butter, it is very moist.

4 EGGS
230G CASTER SUGAR
350G COOKED BEETROOT, PEELED
165ML SUNFLOWER OIL
2 TSP PURE VANILLA EXTRACT
150G PLAIN WHITE FLOUR
1/2 TSP SALT
2 TSP BAKING POWDER
40G COCOA POWDER, PLUS EXTRA
    FOR DUSTING
200G WHITE CHOCOLATE CHUNKS
BUTTER, FOR GREASING

1. Preheat the oven to 160°C. Whisk together the eggs and sugar with an electric mixer until pale and thick.
2. In a food processor, blend the beetroot with the oil and vanilla extract until smooth. 3. Sift the flour, salt, baking powder and cocoa powder into a bowl.
4. Whisk the beetroot into the egg and sugar mix, then gently fold in the sifted dry ingredients. Mix in the white chocolate.
5. Butter a 28cm cake tin with a removable bottom and line the bottom with baking parchment. Line the side of the tin with a separate strip of parchment. 6. Pour in the cake mixture. Bake for 40–50 minutes until a skewer inserted into the centre comes out clean. Allow to cool. 7. When cold, remove the cake from the tin. Dust the top with cocoa powder.

## VICTORIA SPONGE
*Makes a 25cm cake*

The classic British sandwich cake, this was – as you would expect – named in honour of Queen Victoria. We haven't tinkered with it and ours is quite traditional, being light but firm and filled with good jam and whipped unsweetened cream.

**250G SOFT BUTTER**
**250G CASTER SUGAR**
**4 EGGS**
**250G PLAIN WHITE FLOUR**
**2 TSP BAKING POWDER**
**20G ICING SUGAR FOR DUSTING**

FILLING
**80G RASPBERRY OR STRAWBERRY JAM**
**150ML DOUBLE CREAM, WHIPPED**

**1.** Preheat the oven to 170°C. Beat the butter with the caster sugar until pale and fluffy. **2.** In a bowl, whisk the eggs just to mix. Slowly add the eggs to the butter and sugar mix, making sure each addition is well mixed in before adding more. **3.** Sift the flour and baking powder, then gently fold into the egg mix with a spatula. **4.** Use baking parchment to line the bottom of a 25cm round cake tin with a removable bottom. Line the side of the tin with a separate strip of parchment. Pour in the cake mixture. **5.** Bake for 30–35 minutes until a skewer inserted into the centre of the cake comes out clean. Cool on a wire rack. **6.** Remove the cake from the tin and split into two equal layers using a bread knife. **7.** Spread jam on the cut surface of one layer and whipped cream on the other cut surface. Sandwich together. Dust the top of the cake with icing sugar.

## SHORTBREAD
*Makes 15–20 fingers*

Rich and buttery, these just melt in your mouth, as proper shortbread should. If you have stored them in a tin, warm them ever so slightly in the oven before eating, to bring out the butteriness.

**420G PLAIN WHITE FLOUR**
**1/2 TSP BAKING POWDER**
**225G COLD BUTTER**
**180G VANILLA CASTER SUGAR**

**1.** Sift the flour and baking powder into the bowl of an electric mixer. Cut the butter into cubes and toss with the flour. Leave for 30 minutes. **2.** Turn on the mixer and process until the mixture forms crumbs. Add the sugar and continue processing until the mix starts to form small lumps. **3.** Tip into a 30 x 20cm baking tin lined with greaseproof paper. Spread out the mix and press down into an even layer. Chill for 1 hour. **4.** Preheat the oven to 180°C. **5.** Bake the shortbread for 18–20 minutes until set and very light golden. **6.** While still hot, cut into fingers. Leave to cool in the tin. Store in an airtight container.

## CHOCOLATE AND PECAN BROWNIES
*Makes 12 brownies*

The Canteen brownie is squidgy in the middle, not cakey. To achieve this, it's important not to overcook and follow conventional cake-testing directions. Use good-quality chocolate for the richest flavour – we use Valrhona.

**225G DARK CHOCOLATE**
     **(70% COCOA SOLIDS)**
**2 EGGS**
**2 EGG YOLKS**
**110G PLAIN WHITE FLOUR**
**70G COCOA POWDER**
**1/2 TSP BAKING POWDER**
**1/2 TSP SALT**
**225G SOFT BUTTER**
**200G CASTER SUGAR**
**120G PECAN NUT HALVES**

**1.** Preheat the oven to 160°C. Break the chocolate into a heatproof bowl and set over a pan of simmering water to melt. **2.** Beat the eggs and yolks together. **3.** Sift the flour, cocoa powder, baking powder and salt into a bowl. **4.** In another bowl, beat the butter with the sugar until pale and fluffy. Slowly mix in the eggs and then the melted chocolate. Fold in the sifted dry ingredients and half of the pecans. **5.** Use baking parchment to line a 30 x 20cm cake tin, 6cm deep. Tip the chocolate mixture into the tin and spread out evenly. **6.** Bake for 16 minutes, then test with the tip of a knife – it should come out with bits stuck to it, but not runny cake mixture. **7.** Allow to cool, then cut into squares.

NOTE: Instead of pecans, use toasted halved hazelnuts.

## CARROT CAKE
*Serves 6–8*

Although usually thought of as American, carrot cakes and puddings have a very long history in Britain. Canteen's recipe for carrot cake is moist and quite spicy with a generous layer of soft-cheese icing. It's incredibly popular with our afternoon tea-and-cake customers.

**400G CASTER SUGAR**
**300ML SUNFLOWER OIL**
**2 WHOLE EGGS**
**2 EGGS, SEPARATED**
**150G GRATED CARROTS**
**300G SELF-RAISING WHITE**
**   FLOUR**
**1/2 TSP BICARBONATE OF SODA**
**150G WALNUTS, ROUGHLY**
**   CHOPPED**
**1 TSP GROUND CINNAMON**
**1/2 TSP GROUND MACE**
**1/2 TSP FRESHLY GRATED NUTMEG**
**1 TSP GROUND GINGER**
**GRATED ZEST OF 1 ORANGE**

ICING
**250G SOFT BUTTER**
**300G ICING SUGAR**
**500G FULL-FAT SOFT CHEESE**

**1.** Preheat the oven to 180°C. Whisk together the caster sugar, oil, eggs and yolks with an electric mixer until pale and thick. **2.** Stir in the carrots. **3.** Sift the flour with the bicarbonate of soda. Fold into the whisked mixture together with the walnuts, spices and orange zest. **4.** Whisk the egg whites in a clean bowl until stiff. Fold into the cake mixture. **5.** Use baking parchment to line a 30 x 20cm cake tin that is 6cm deep. Spoon in the cake mixture. **6.** Bake for 35–40 minutes until a skewer inserted into the centre comes out clean. Cool on a wire rack in the tin. **7.** To make the icing, beat the butter with the sugar until pale and fluffy. Add the soft cheese and beat for a further 20 seconds. **8.** Spread the icing over the top of the cake and roughen the surface with a fork. Chill for 1 hour. Cut into squares for serving.

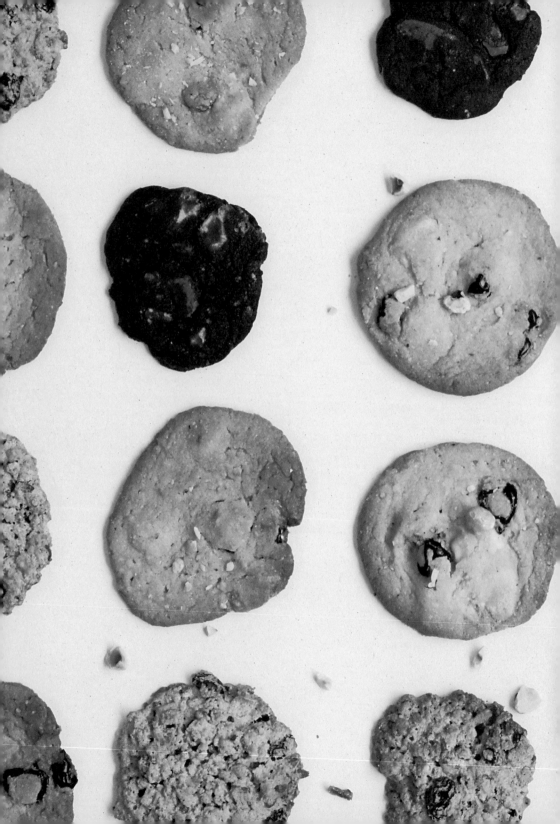

## HAZELNUT, CHERRY AND WHITE CHOCOLATE COOKIES
*Makes 12–15*

These are really easy and fun to make with your kids. As with most cookies, if you want them to have a soft texture take them out of the oven when they are browned just at the edges – they'll continue to cook and set on the hot baking sheet.

- 150G TOASTED HAZELNUTS, CHOPPED
- 2 TSP SUNFLOWER OIL
- 1/2 TSP SALT
- 1 TSP PURE VANILLA EXTRACT
- 70G BUTTER
- 50G CASTER SUGAR
- 100G MUSCOVADO SUGAR
- 1 EGG
- 150G PLAIN WHITE FLOUR
- 1 TSP BAKING POWDER
- 75G WHITE CHOCOLATE CHIPS
- 50G DRIED CHERRIES

1. Preheat the oven to 175°C. Put 100g of the hazelnuts in a food processor with the oil, salt and vanilla. Blend until smooth. 2. Beat together the nut mixture, butter, caster and muscovado sugars and egg in a bowl. Mix in all the other ingredients along with the remaining nuts. 3. Divide into walnut-sized pieces and arrange, well spaced out, on a non-stick baking sheet or a tray lined with baking parchment. 4. Bake for 6–7 minutes until light golden brown around the edges. 5. Leave to cool and set on the tray for 15 minutes before removing to a wire rack to cool completely. Store in an airtight tin.

## CHOCOLATE CHIP COOKIES
*Makes about 30*

Reputed to be an aphrodisiac, a stimulant and addictive, chocolate is one of the most ancient sweet treats. There's no doubt it gives comfort and pleasure. This triple-chocolate cookie will certainly satisfy your cravings.

- 220G SOFT BUTTER
- 100G CASTER SUGAR
- 220G MUSCOVADO SUGAR
- 2 EGGS
- 2 TSP PURE VANILLA EXTRACT
- 280G PLAIN WHITE FLOUR
- 60G COCOA POWDER
- 1 TSP SALT
- 1 TSP BAKING POWDER
- 250G MILK CHOCOLATE CHIPS
- 250G WHITE CHOCOLATE, CUT IN CHUNKS

1. Preheat the oven to 175°C. Cream the butter with the caster and muscovado sugars until pale and fluffy. 2. Add the eggs and vanilla extract and beat in thoroughly. 3. Sift the flour, cocoa, salt and baking powder into the bowl and mix well together. Mix in the chocolate chips and chunks. 4. Divide into walnut-sized balls and arrange, well spaced out, on a non-stick baking sheet or a sheet lined with baking parchment. Bake for 6–7 minutes until set around the edges but still soft in the centre. 5. Leave to cool and set on the tray for 15 minutes before removing to a wire rack to cool completely. Store in an airtight tin.

## MUESLI COOKIES

*Makes about 20*

These are good, crunchy flapjacky cookies. Use your favourite muesli – it doesn't matter if it has lots of fruit or nuts, or contains more oats and other grains. Any muesli will do.

**125G SOFT BUTTER**
**100G MUSCOVADO SUGAR**
**60G CASTER SUGAR**
**1 EGG**
**2 TSP PURE VANILLA EXTRACT**
**300G MUESLI**
**25G SELF-RAISING WHITE FLOUR**
**BIG PINCH OF SALT**

**1.** Preheat the oven to 160°C. Beat the butter with the muscovado and caster sugars until pale and fluffy. **2.** Beat in the egg, followed by the vanilla extract and 4½ tablespoons water. Mix in the muesli, flour and salt. **3.** Roll into walnut-sized balls and arrange, well spaced apart, on a non-stick baking sheet or a sheet lined with baking parchment. Flatten each ball slightly. **4.** Bake for about 15 minutes or until golden brown. **5.** Leave to cool and set on the sheet for 15 minutes before removing to a wire rack to cool completely. Store in an airtight tin.

## PEANUT BUTTER COOKIES

*Makes 15–20*

Both sweet and a bit salty, our Canteen peanut butter cookies have a satisfyingly dense, coarse texture from the inclusion of porridge oats and chopped nuts.

**75G SOFT BUTTER**
**110G MUSCOVADO SUGAR**
**90G CASTER SUGAR**
**1 EGG**
**1 TSP PURE VANILLA EXTRACT**
**120G PEANUT BUTTER (EITHER SMOOTH OR CRUNCHY)**
**75G PORRIDGE OATS**
**80G ROASTED SALTED PEANUTS, CHOPPED**
**60G PLAIN WHOLEMEAL FLOUR**
**1 TSP BICARBONATE OF SODA**

**1.** Preheat the oven to 165°C. Cream the butter with the muscovado and caster sugars until pale and fluffy. **2.** Add the egg and vanilla extract and mix well. **3.** Mix in all the other ingredients. **4.** Divide into walnut-sized balls and arrange, well spaced apart, on a non-stick baking sheet or a sheet lined with baking parchment. Flatten the balls slightly. Bake for about 8 minutes or until golden brown. **5.** Leave to cool and set on the sheet for 15 minutes before removing to a wire rack to cool completely. Store in an airtight tin.

NOTE: Try cashews instead of chopped peanuts.

## CHAPTER 6

# BASICS AND MISC.

## MEAT STOCK

If you have room in your freezer, keep all your carrot, onion, celery and leek peelings and trimmings plus fresh herb stalks. Pack in bags and store until you have a couple of bagsful, then make stock. (If you don't have any vegetable trimmings when you want to make stock, use 1 small onion, 2 celery sticks, 1 carrot and 1 leek, all roughly chopped.) Bones from roasts can be kept in the freezer too.

> **BONES FROM ROASTS (SEE BELOW)**
> **PARSLEY, SAGE, THYME AND**
>   **ROSEMARY STALKS**
> **ONION, LEEK, CARROT AND**
>   **CELERY PEELINGS AND**
>   **TRIMMINGS**
> **20 BLACK PEPPERCORNS**
> **6 BAY LEAVES**
> **ANY JUICES AND SCRAPINGS**
>   **FROM ROASTS**

1. Place everything in a big pot, cover with cold water and bring to the boil. Turn down to the lowest heat possible and skim off any fat with a ladle. Simmer for 2–3 hours. 2. Pour the liquid through a fine strainer set in a bowl. Discard the bones, vegetables and flavourings. Pour the stock back into the pot and bring to the boil. Reduce by half or until you have a good strong and meaty-tasting stock.

NOTES: A mixture of bones from roast chicken, beef and pork makes a rich, full-flavoured stock • For a lighter chicken stock, use just roast chicken bones. You can freeze the reduced stock for later use • When we want a Vegetable stock, we make it up with Marigold vegetable bouillon powder.

## ONION GRAVY
*Makes 400–500ml*

> **2 TBSP OLIVE OIL**
> **25G BUTTER**
> **800G ONIONS, THINLY SLICED**
> **200G SHALLOTS, THINLY SLICED**
> **4 GARLIC CLOVES, CHOPPED**
> **10G FRESH THYME LEAVES,**
>   **CHOPPED**
> **10G FRESH ROSEMARY LEAVES,**
>   **CHOPPED**
> **1 LITRE MEAT STOCK (P202)**
> **1 TSP SALT**
> **150ML RED WINE**
> **50ML SHERRY VINEGAR**
> **1 1/2 TBSP CORNFLOUR**

1. Heat up the oil in a large pan until hot. Add the butter with the onions and shallots and cook on a high heat, stirring frequently, for 15 minutes or until starting to brown. Reduce the heat and continue cooking for about 1 hour or until soft and caramelised, stirring frequently. 2. Add the garlic and chopped herbs. Cook for a further 15 minutes, then add the meat stock and salt. 3. Put the wine and vinegar into a small pan and bring to the boil. Reduce by three-quarters. 4. Add the wine reduction to the onion mix. Bring to the boil and simmer for 30 minutes, stirring occasionally. 5. Mix the cornflour with a little cold water and stir into the gravy. Bring back to the boil to thicken. Check the seasoning, then serve hot.

NOTES: You can make the gravy ahead of time and reheat it for serving. It also freezes well for 1–2 months – just heat from frozen until boiling • For a vegetarian onion gravy, substitute Vegetable stock (see opposite) for the meat stock.

## HOLLANDAISE SAUCE
*Serves 4*

**250G UNSALTED BUTTER**
**4 EGG YOLKS**
**I TSP TARRAGON VINEGAR**
**PINCH OF SALT**
**$1/2$ LEMON**
**CAYENNE PEPPER**

**I.** Melt the butter on a low heat. It will separate to make a layer of clear golden fat (clarified butter) on top. Use a ladle to remove the clarified butter, leaving the milky residue in the pan (discard the residue). Keep the clarified butter in a warm place. **2.** Put the egg yolks in a stainless-steel bowl with the vinegar, salt and 2 teaspoons cold water and whisk for a few minutes. **3.** Set the bowl over a pan of simmering water. **4.** Continue whisking until the mixture is pale, thick and fluffy. **5.** Remove from the pan of simmering water and slowly whisk in the clarified butter. Squeeze in the lemon juice, season with a pinch of cayenne and check the salt. Serve as soon as possible.

NOTE: When making hollandaise, keep the butter wrapper. Then if you need to keep the sauce for a bit before serving, you can place the wrapper on the surface of the sauce, to keep it warm and prevent a skin from forming.

## MAYONNAISE
*Makes about 300ml*

**2 TSP DIJON MUSTARD**
**2 TSP WHITE WINE VINEGAR**
**$1/2$ TSP SALT**
**2 EGG YOLKS**
**300ML SUNFLOWER OIL**

**I.** Whisk together the mustard, vinegar, salt and egg yolks for 1 minute. **2.** Slowly add the oil while continuing to whisk. When all the oil is incorporated the mayonnaise should be thick and glossy. Taste and adjust the seasoning, if needed.

NOTES: You can use a balloon whisk, electric mixer or food processor to make the mayonnaise • Home-made mayonnaise can be kept in the fridge for 2 days • For garlic mayonnaise, use lemon juice instead of vinegar, and 150ml each olive and sunflower oils. Add 3 garlic cloves, finely chopped, and the grated zest of a lemon.

## PARSLEY SAUCE
*Serves 6*

Our version of this classic is not just a white sauce with some chopped parsley stirred in. We infuse the milk with the parsley stalks, which gives a much deeper flavour.

**50G FRESH CURLY PARSLEY**
**400ML FULL-FAT MILK**
**200ML DOUBLE CREAM**
**I SMALL ONION, CUT IN HALF**
**2 BAY LEAVES**
**2 WHOLE CLOVES**
**25G BUTTER**
**25G PLAIN WHITE FLOUR**
**PINCH OF FRESHLY GRATED**
  **NUTMEG**
**SALT AND WHITE PEPPER**

**1.** Pick the parsley leaves from the stalks and reserve. Chop the stalks. **2.** Place the milk in a small saucepan with the cream, onion, bay leaves, cloves and parsley stalks. Bring to the boil. When boiling remove from the heat, cover and leave to infuse for 30 minutes. **3.** Strain the liquid and discard the flavourings. **4.** Melt the butter in a saucepan and stir in the flour. Cook, stirring, for 2–3 minutes. Slowly incorporate the hot creamy milk, whisking constantly – only add more of the liquid when you have whisked to the point that the mixture is smooth again. Continue whisking until the sauce is boiling and has thickened. Simmer for 5 minutes. **5.** Remove from the heat and season with the nutmeg and a pinch each of salt and white pepper. **6.** Chop the parsley leaves and stir into the sauce. Serve hot.

NOTES: If you want to make the sauce ahead of time, don't add the chopped parsley leaves. Store in the fridge, then reheat for serving and stir in the parsley at the last minute • This sauce was devised to serve with gammon, which is salty. If you are going to serve it with white fish, for example, you might want to add more salt.

## MUSTARD DRESSING
*Makes about 125ml*

**2 TBSP DIJON MUSTARD**
**1 TSP WHITE WINE VINEGAR**
**1 GARLIC CLOVE, VERY FINELY**
   **CHOPPED**
**100ML SUNFLOWER OIL**
**SALT**

**1.** Whisk together the mustard, vinegar, garlic, salt to taste and 1 tablespoon water in a bowl. **2.** Slowly incorporate the oil, whisking thoroughly. Use straight away or store in the fridge until needed.

NOTE: The dressing can be kept for up to a week in the fridge. Shake it well before using.

## TARTARE SAUCE
*Serves 6*

**50G DRAINED CAPERS**
**60G DRAINED SWEET-PICKLED**
   **GHERKINS**
**10G FRESH TARRAGON**
**20G FRESH CHIVES**
**GRATED ZEST OF 1 LEMON**
**JUICE OF 1/2 LEMON**
**200ML MAYONNAISE (P203)**

**1.** Finely chop the capers and gherkins. Chop the tarragon and chives. **2.** Place all the ingredients in a bowl and mix together. Cover and keep in the fridge until required.

NOTE: The sauce can be kept in the fridge for 2 days.

## SALAD CREAM
*Makes about 500ml*

Commercial brands of salad cream are sweet and glutinous. Ours is far superior and really easy to make. It keeps well and makes a good standby for dressing all kinds of salads.

**30G PLAIN WHITE FLOUR**
**4 TSP ENGLISH MUSTARD POWDER**
**1/2 TSP SALT**
**1/2 TSP WHITE PEPPER**
**40ML OLIVE OIL**
**50G CASTER SUGAR**
**450ML MILK**
**1 EGG**
**200ML CIDER VINEGAR**

**1.** Mix together the flour, mustard powder, salt and pepper. Add the olive oil and sugar and beat well. **2.** Beat together the milk and egg in a saucepan, then add the mustard mixture. Slowly beat in the vinegar. **3.** Set the pan over the heat and bring the mixture to a simmer, stirring constantly. Simmer for 5 minutes. **4.** Allow to cool completely, then store in a tightly closed bottle or jar in the fridge.

NOTE: The salad cream will keep for up to 2 weeks.

## SHERRY VINEGAR DRESSING
*Makes 250ml*

**50ML SHERRY VINEGAR**
**3–4 SPRIGS OF FRESH THYME**
**4 GARLIC CLOVES, CHOPPED**
**BLACK PEPPER**
**200ML OLIVE OIL**

1. Put all the ingredients into a bottle or screwtop jar. Cover and shake well to emulsify. 2. Use straight away or store until needed.

NOTE: The dressing can be kept for up to a week in the fridge. Shake it well before using.

## CUSTARD
*Makes about 1 litre to serve 6*

**750ML FULL-FAT MILK**
**250ML DOUBLE CREAM**
**I VANILLA POD, SPLIT OPEN**
   **LENGTHWAYS**
**3 EGG YOLKS**
**60G CASTER SUGAR**
**25G CORNFLOUR**

1. Place the milk, cream and vanilla pod in a pan and bring to the boil. 2. Whisk together the egg yolks, sugar and cornflour in a bowl. Pour over the boiling liquid, stirring well. 3. Pour into a clean pan and heat gently, stirring, until the custard has thickened. Discard the vanilla pod before serving.

## SHORT PASTRY
*Makes a 25cm tart case*

**200G PLAIN WHITE FLOUR, PLUS**
   **EXTRA FOR DUSTING**
**1/2 TSP SALT**
**100G COLD BUTTER, CUT IN CUBES,**
   **PLUS EXTRA FOR GREASING**
**I WHOLE EGG, BEATEN WITH A**
   **SPLASH OF COLD WATER**
**I EGG YOLK, BEATEN**

1. Place the flour and salt in a bowl. Rub the butter into the flour with your fingertips until you have a fine crumb consistency. 2. Add half of the beaten whole egg and mix well to bring together into a dough. If too dry, add more of the egg as needed. Shape into a ball, wrap in cling film and chill in the fridge for 1 hour. 3. To make the tart case, use softened butter to grease a 25cm tart tin with a removable bottom and fluted sides. Sprinkle in some flour to coat, then tip out the excess. 4. Roll out the pastry dough on a well-floured cool surface to a round about 2mm thick that is slightly bigger than the tart tin. Roll up the pastry sheet around the rolling pin and lay it over the tin. Ease in to line the bottom and sides, ensuring it goes right into the corners. Trim off excess pastry, leaving about 1cm overhang. Prick the tart case all over with a fork. Chill for 30 minutes. 5. Preheat the oven to 175°C. Line the tart case with baking parchment and fill with baking beans or dried pulses. Bake for 12 minutes. 6. Remove the beans and parchment. Reduce the heat to 130°C and bake for a further 12 minutes. 7. Brush the beaten egg yolk all over the pastry. Place back in the oven to bake for a final 2 minutes – this is to seal the base to prevent any leaks of filling.

## SWEET PASTRY
*Makes a 25cm tart case*

**100G BUTTER, DICED, PLUS
    EXTRA FOR GREASING
150G PLAIN WHITE FLOUR, PLUS
    EXTRA FOR DUSTING
PINCH OF SALT
45G CASTER SUGAR
2 EGG YOLKS**

1. Mix the butter with the flour, salt and sugar, rubbing gently with the tips of your fingers until the mixture is like fine crumbs. 2. Whisk one of the egg yolks with 1 tablespoon cold water. Slowly add to the butter and flour, mixing with your fingertips until it forms a dough. Add 1 teaspoon more water if needed. 3. Shape into a ball and wrap in cling film. Chill for at least 1 hour. 4. To make the tart case, use softened butter to grease a 25cm tart tin with a removable bottom and fluted sides. Sprinkle in some flour to coat all over, then tip out the excess. 5. Roll out the dough on a well-floured cool surface to a round that is slightly larger than the tin. 6. Gently roll the sheet of dough around the pin and lay it over the tin. Ease in to line the bottom and sides. Trim off excess pastry dough, leaving a 1cm overhang. Prick the tart case all over, then chill for 30 minutes. 7. Preheat the oven to 175°C. Line the tart case with baking parchment and fill with baking beans or dried pulses. Bake for 14 minutes. 8. Remove the beans and parchment. Lower the heat to 135°C and bake for a further 15–20 minutes until the pastry has dried out and is light golden brown. 9. Beat the remaining egg yolk and brush all over the pastry. Place back in the oven to bake for a final 2 minutes – this is to seal the base to prevent any leaks of filling.

## PICKLED SHALLOTS
*Makes about 600g*

**600G BANANA SHALLOTS, PEELED
1/2 TSP SALT
250ML RED WINE VINEGAR
150G SUGAR
2 BAY LEAVES
10 BLACK PEPPERCORNS**

1. Slice the shallots on a mandoline into thin rings (don't throw away the trimmings). Toss with the salt in a stainless-steel bowl. 2. Combine the vinegar, sugar, bay leaves, peppercorns and 2 litres water in a stainless-steel pan and bring to the boil. 3. Pour the vinegar mixture over the shallots and mix well. Cover with cling film and cool. Store in the fridge (in the stainless-steel bowl or glass jars). 4. To serve, spoon out the shallots and drain off the vinegar.

NOTES: The shallots can be kept in the fridge for up to a month • You can use the vinegar to make Mint sauce (p138) or a variation of Sherry vinegar dressing (p207).

## BEETROOT RELISH
*Makes enough to fill two 500g jars*

**200G RED ONIONS, PEELED**
**600G COOKED BEETROOT, PEELED**
**75ML SHERRY VINEGAR**
**1 TSP SALT**
**50G CASTER SUGAR**
**100ML ORANGE JUICE**
**1/2 TSP GROUND GINGER**

1. Place the red onions in a food processor and blend or chop finely (you want small pieces but not a purée). 2. Do the same with the beetroot. 3. Combine all the ingredients in a stainless-steel pan and cook on a low heat for 45 minutes, stirring frequently. Allow to cool. 4. Ladle into sterilised jars and close tightly. Store in the fridge.

NOTE: The relish can be kept for up to a month.

## APPLE CHUTNEY
*Makes enough to fill three 500g jars*

**1KG BRAMLEY APPLES**
**500G ONIONS, DICED**
**400G CAN CHOPPED TOMATOES**
**300ML CIDER VINEGAR**
**300ML ORANGE JUICE**
**150G DRIED CHOPPED APPLES**
**2 TSP GROUND ALLSPICE**
**1 TSP GROUND GINGER**
**1 TSP GROUND MACE**
**1 TSP MUSTARD SEEDS**
**400G CASTER SUGAR**

1. Peel the apples, remove the cores and cut into small chunks. 2. Place everything except the sugar in a preserving pan or other wide, deep pan. Bring just to the boil, then simmer for 2 hours, stirring frequently. 3. Add the sugar and stir well. Continue cooking over a low heat for 1 hour, stirring frequently. 4. Ladle into sterilised jars while still hot. When completely cold, store in a cool, dark place.

NOTES: The chutney can be kept for up to 6 months, and will improve as it matures. Once a jar is opened, keep it in the fridge • For pear chutney, replace the apples with the same weight of pears that are hard and not too ripe.

## PICCALILLI

*Makes enough to fill three 500g jars*

Everyone loves our piccalilli, which is sweeter than the traditional version of this mighty condiment. The combination of sweet mustard and turmeric-spiced pickled vegetables is very good.

**I SMALL CAULIFLOWER**
**200G GREEN BEANS**
**I RED PEPPER, CUT IN ICM DICE**
**I ONION, CUT IN ICM DICE**
**2 TSP SALT**
**250ML WHITE WINE VINEGAR**
**I TSP TURMERIC**
**1/2 TSP GROUND GINGER**
**2 TSP BLACK MUSTARD SEEDS**
**200G CASTER SUGAR**
**80G PLAIN WHITE FLOUR**
**4 TSP ENGLISH MUSTARD POWDER**

**1.** Cut the cauliflower into small florets, including some of the stalk. Cut the green beans into 1-cm lengths. **2.** Combine the cauliflower, beans, red pepper and onion in a bowl. Sprinkle with the salt and leave for 12 hours. **3.** Place the vegetables in a stainless-steel pan with the vinegar, 250ml water, the turmeric, ginger and mustard seeds. Cover and bring to the boil, then simmer for 5–10 minutes (the cauliflower should still be firm). **4.** Drain the vegetables in a sieve set over a bowl. Reserve the vegetables. Return the liquid to the pan and add the sugar. Bring to the boil, stirring to dissolve the sugar. **5.** Put the flour and mustard powder in a bowl that is big enough to contain the boiling liquid. Add 75ml cold water and stir to make a paste. Pour in the boiling liquid, whisking well. Return to the pan and keep stirring on a low to medium heat until the mixture boils. **6.** Remove from the heat and mix in the vegetables. Allow to cool, then ladle into sterilised jars. Keep in the fridge.

NOTES: Piccalilli can be eaten straight away, but will improve in flavour after a few days · It can be kept in the fridge for up to 6 months.

## MARMALADE
*Makes about 2kg*

**IKG SEVILLE ORANGES**
**2KG SUGAR**

**1.** Cut the oranges in half and squeeze out the juice; reserve the juice. With a spoon, scrape out any pips from the orange halves and keep these too. **2.** Cut the orange skins in half again, then cut into strips – thick or thin, depending on how you like it. Place the strips in a non-reactive pan with the juice and 700ml water. **3.** Wrap the pips and any other scrapings in a square of muslin and tie up well (if this is not secure you may end up with marmalade that's full of pips). Add this to the pan. Cover and leave overnight. **4.** The next day, place the pan on the stove and bring to the boil. Cook for 1–1½ hours until the orange strips are translucent and soft. During the cooking be sure to stir very frequently to prevent the marmalade from sticking to the bottom of the pan and burning. At the same time press the bag with the spoon to squeeze out the natural pectin that is in the pips. **5.** Place a few saucers in the freezer ready for the testing. **6.** When the orange strips are soft, add the sugar and stir well to dissolve. Cook on a rolling boil on a medium heat for a further 45 minutes. **7.** To test for set, pour a little of the marmalade syrup on to one of the cold plates and leave for a few minutes, then push it gently with your finger. If the marmalade wrinkles it is ready. If not, cook for a further 15 minutes and test again. **8.** Ladle into sterilised jars while still hot. When completely cold, store in a cool, dark place.

## RASPBERRY JAM
*Makes enough to fill two 500g jars*

**500G RASPBERRIES**
**500G PRESERVING SUGAR**
  **(CONTAINS PECTIN)**
**JUICE OF I ORANGE**

**1.** Place all the ingredients in a stainless-steel saucepan and bring to the boil on a low heat, stirring frequently to prevent burning. Cook for 30 minutes. The pectin in the preserving sugar will guarantee a set. **2.** Ladle into sterilised jars while still hot. When completely cold, store in a cool, dark place.

## CONVERSION CHARTS

### SPOON MEASURES

Spoon measurements are level unless otherwise specified.

1 teaspoon (tsp) = 5ml
1 tablespoon (tbsp) = 15ml

### OVEN TEMPERATURES

| FAN °C | °C | °F | GAS |
|---|---|---|---|
| 90 | 110 | 225 | ¼ |
| 100 | 120 | 250 | ½ |
| 120 | 100 | 275 | 1 |
| 130 | 150 | 300 | 2 |
| 140 | 160 | 325 | 3 |
| 160 | 180 | 350 | 4 |
| 170 | 190 | 375 | 5 |
| 180 | 200 | 400 | 6 |
| 200 | 220 | 425 | 7 |
| 210 | 230 | 450 | 8 |
| 220 | 240 | 475 | 9 |

### VOLUME MEASURES

| METRIC | IMPERIAL |
|---|---|
| 25ml | 1fl oz |
| 50ml | 2fl oz |
| 100ml | 3½fl oz |
| 120ml | 4fl oz |
| 150ml | 5fl oz (¼ pint) |
| 175ml | 6fl oz |
| 200ml | 7fl oz |
| 250ml | 8fl oz |
| 300ml | 10fl oz (½ pint) |
| 450ml | 15fl oz |
| 600ml | 20fl oz (1 pint) |
| 1 litre | 35fl oz (1¾ pints) |

### LINEAR MEASURES

| METRIC | IMPERIAL |
|---|---|
| 3mm | ⅛ inch |
| 5mm | ¼ inch |
| 1cm | ½ inch |
| 2cm | ¾ inch |
| 2.5cm | 1 inch |
| 5cm | 2 inch |
| 10cm | 4 inch |
| 20cm | 8 inch |
| 30cm | 12 inch |

### WEIGHTS

| METRIC | IMPERIAL |
|---|---|
| 5g | ⅛oz |
| 10g | ¼oz |
| 15g | ½oz |
| 25g | 1oz |
| 40g | 1½oz |
| 50g | 2oz |
| 75g | 3oz |
| 100g | 4oz (¼lb) |
| 120g | 4½oz |
| 150g | 5oz |
| 175g | 6oz |
| 200g | 7oz |
| 225g | 8oz (½lb) |
| 250g | 9oz |
| 275g | 10oz |
| 300g | 11oz |
| 350g | 12oz (¾lb) |
| 375g | 13oz |
| 400g | 14oz |
| 425g | 15oz |
| 450g | 1lb (16oz) |
| 550g | 1¼lb |
| 750g | 1½lb |
| 1kg | 2¼lb |

## COOK'S NOTES

All the recipes in the book have been adapted for the home cook and domestic kitchen, and tested by Cass at home (with Patrick as the official taster).

We prefer to use organic eggs, milk and other dairy products, poultry and meat, but the decision is, of course, up to you. Unless otherwise specified in a recipe:

**BUTTER IS UNSALTED**
**EGGS ARE LARGE**
**SALT IS FINE SEA SALT**
**PEPPER IS BLACK PEPPER**

Oven temperatures given in recipes are for a fan oven. If you are using a conventional oven, add 20°C to the temperature specified. For a chart of equivalent oven temperatures, including gas marks, see opposite.

## ACKNOWLEDGEMENTS

Thank you for the tireless efforts of all who have worked with and for Canteen. Very special thank you to all those that invested in us. Special thank you to Sarah Lavelle: you're a star.

Thank you to Polly Barnes for your leap of faith and tireless efforts. Special Ops Commander Tom Gell, we salute you.

### PATRICK

Hank (very sadly missed, never forgotten, a brightly shining star).

The Best Mum, Tim, gorgeous LISA, wonderful sister Claire, James, Agnes, Dudley, special thoughts to Kate, Charlie and Tullula, Staiteman for being a superstar, Sophie Titcombe for being ace, Zoe, Russell and Hope, Will, Luella and Mila, Bernie, Penny-Bell and Willow, James Miles, Thea, Ben Dangerous and Maggi, Matt and Jason, Tooni, Rita Meter Maid, Susie Millns, Josh (NJ) Millns, Chris stoffer (the claw) Lawson, Ric, Anna and the twins, Lucia, Richard and the best godson ever, superhero Dexter, Kirsty and Simon, Tommo (Cheddar cheese balls), Jessica, Adam and the Hynes clan, Karen Morfill, Lucy-May and Keirin, Richard Blair, Sarah Fung, Angela Hartnett, Shane Osborn, Mark for his Northern stamp of approval, Myke Vince, Senor Bignose, Achingbrain, Alex G, the King of New York, Jane and Jamie, Adam and Tieu, Anna and Leo, Bill Knots, Rebecca Seal, Polly Vernon, Paul Croughton, John Coyne, Sean Hamilton, Tony Turnnall, Paul Henderson, Joe Mott, Antie M, Sandra and Andy, Alison and Huge, Cousin Helen, Stefano, Alexia, Chiara, Sienna and Athena, Phil Westaby, Celine and Jonny, Jonno, Grumpy Graham, Green eggs on ham, Don at the Bell, Ian Wood, Steve Henwood, Clare, Marion, Nicky, Will, Pizza Jo, Emma, Joe and Zoe, Dave, Sidsel, Steve, Chris and Iona 'isokon' McCourt, Angela Moore and Sarah May, Mark Simpson, Ed, Jay, Clare and Hannah at Universal, Rocksteady 'forecourt Eddie' (Ed Carpenter), Dr Dre (Andre Klauser), Charles Campion, Fay Maschler, Adrian Gill, Jay Rayner, Giles Coren, Hugo Macdonald, Tony Chambers, Bloomberg, Alexa Chung, Margaret Howell, Nicolas Chandor, Paul and Lisa Gilligan, Simon Alderson, Tony Cunningham, Sophie, Eva, Mia, Lauren, Veronica and all Twentytwentyone crew and their oasis of courtyard calm, Kevin Allan, Karti, Charlie and Gabriel, Richard Shed, Bethan Rider, Luke Powell for his super-graphic jiggery-pokery and general brilliance, Jodie, Jethro, Marie-France Kittler, Bill Bragg, Laura Housley, Antonia Ward, Nick Lander, Anne Hines, Sheila King, Marc Voulters, Susie Footitt, Brent at Meantime, Randolph, Patrick and Jason at Neal's Yard Dairy, Vernon at Secretts, Joseph Muller Brockman, Phil, Tessa and Charlie at Taste, Graham, Stuart, Brian and all at City Beverage, Anita at Monmouth Coffee, Kalavinka Bikes, Sheldon Brown, Paul Smith, Robin and Lucienne Day, Lance Armstrong, Don Letts, Hewy, Graham Coxon, Dizzee Rascal, Adam and Joe, Rebecca, Angela, Ray, Simon, Carl, John, Matthew, Jarrod, Richard, Mike, Tim, Tamara, Debbie, Tanya, Dingle, Harry, Sarah, Debbie, Daniel, Andy, Caroline, Mark, Helen, Mr Hannah, Dick The Fish, Mrs White, Miranda, Owen and Mary, and anyone missed off by mistake: thank you.

### DOM

Anki Lake for the positivity and sunshine she brought from day one to fuel the Canteen dream. Anita Lake for her strength, support and encouragement to go for it. Coat-hanger Pete for lessons learnt under his tutorage. All investors in Canteen for their belief in three guys with an idea. Brent Smith at Meantime for his unwavering support of Canteen. Paul Gilligan, a valued mentor and advisor for his passion and belief in us. Marc Voulters for commercial guidance and a safe pair of hands. The team at Canteen who make it happen – yeah! Tony for great grass-fed additive free beef, dry-aged for over 28 days. Paddy Plunkett at Neal's Yard for wonderful cheese. John Mullins at The London Business school for writing a great book, *What to Do Before Writing a Business Plan*, which we used successfully.

### CASS

My mum and dad, who started it all. To my kids, Tabby and Oscar, for being my biggest fans and suffering all the demands of having a dad who spends far too much time in the kitchen. All the team at Baker Street for putting up with many days of photoshoots, especially Hugo for the abundance of cakes and Miguel for the pie fiesta. Tim Mawn aka Mawnballs for being a generally all-round good chap, great chef and, last but not least, for the roast squash, fennel and spelt. Tony at Natural Farms for supplying us with some amazing meat! Neal's Yard for the great British cheeses. Matt and Jane at Brighton and Newhaven fish sales for sending me the freshest fish for nearly ten years. Special thanks to Paul and Martin for picking up the phone and putting up with my constant demands for gurnard! Alex Spink and sons for the supply of lovely smoked fish from the East coast of Scotland. Richard Woodall for all things pig. Charlie at our mash purveyors. Angela and Sarah for the photos. All of Canteen's customers.

## BIOGRAPHIES

### ANGELA MOORE

Angela is a London-based photographer who specialises in still life and interiors. Her work includes commissions for Swarovski, the V&A and Frieze Art Fair, and has appeared in publications such as *Elle Decoration*, *Saturday Telegraph* and the *New York Times* magazine. Her work has been exhibited in Vienna, Thessaloniki and London.

### HUDSON-POWELL

Hudson-Powell is a graphic design studio formed by brothers Jody and Luke. With foresight of current and future technologies and a traditional design methodology, they create projects that live across a wide range of media. This approach has seen projects as varied as branding, book design, motion graphics, model making, program development, interactive installations and type design. Hudson-Powell's work has been shown in 'Brno Echo' at the Moravian Gallery (CZ), 'Forms of Inquiry' (UK, FR, CH), and in the solo show 'Responsive Type' at SoSo gallery (JP).